Dallas –

Ro great thing
a blast doing it!

Cheers!
Tod
Orwan

**NEVER KICK
A COW CHIP
ON A HOT DAY**

D1561805

NEVER KICK A COW CHIP ON A HOT DAY

REAL LESSONS FOR REAL CEOS AND THOSE WHO WANT TO BE

TODD ORDAL

New York

NEVER KICK A COW CHIP ON A HOT DAY

REAL LESSONS FOR REAL CEOS AND THOSE WHO WANT TO BE

Published in New York, New York, by Morgan James Publishing. Morgan James and The Entrepreneurial Publisher are trademarks of Morgan James, LLC.
www.MorganJamesPublishing.com

The Morgan James Speakers Group can bring authors to your live event. For more information or to book an event visit The Morgan James Speakers Group at www.TheMorganJamesSpeakersGroup.com.

A **free** eBook edition is available
with the purchase of this print book.

CLEARLY PRINT YOUR NAME ABOVE IN UPPER CASE

Instructions to claim your free eBook edition:
1. Download the BitLit app for Android or iOS
2. Write your name in **UPPER CASE** on the line
3. Use the BitLit app to submit a photo
4. Download your eBook to any device

ISBN 978-1-63047-720-2 paperback
ISBN 978-1-63047-722-6 hardcover
Library of Congress Control Number:
2015912339

Cover Design by:
Rachel Lopez
www.r2cdesign.com

Interior Design by:
Bonnie Bushman
The Whole Caboodle Graphic Design

In an effort to support local communities and raise awareness and funds, Morgan James Publishing donates a percentage of all book sales for the life of each book to Habitat for Humanity Peninsula and Greater Williamsburg.

Get involved today, visit
www.MorganJamesBuilds.com

Habitat
for Humanity®
Peninsula and
Greater Williamsburg
Building Partner

TABLE OF CONTENTS

ACKNOWLEDGMENTS

While I am most often employed to help a CEO lead better, profit more, or just sleep more soundly at night, I would gleefully like to acknowledge that I learn as much from them as they do from me. I have had wonderful clients and would like to thank them for their curiosity, strength, and resilience.

I also learn a great deal from my wife and children. I'm a business junky, but their sense of humor and support are more important than any profit and loss statement I've ever seen!

DEAR READER

For CEOs, it is leaders like Steve Jobs, Jack Welsh, Lee Iacocca, Donald Trump and Mark Zuckerberg who have painted a colorful picture of how to lead. The highs, the lows, the good decisions, and the enormous controversy that follows many of these people often provides us with as much bad guidance on leadership as good. But as leaders we are given, almost destined with, an amazing responsibility. As leaders, we are gifted with the opportunity to be an integral and constant force in the lives of those that we lead. We can shape lives, build opportunities, and hopefully increase the bottom line along the way.

While the stories of the rise and fall of the mighty offer some enormously valuable lessons for all leaders, the implied message is that you too can be the next Steve or Donald or Mark. The most influential leaders in the world likely learned their skills and abilities directly from the school of hard knocks. They fought hard, worked hard, and did all that was needed to overcome the obstacles in their paths. As a leader, we can expect extreme highs, some pretty substantial lows, and a roller coaster ride along the way. But it doesn't always have to be that way: There are opportunities to learn, educate, and enhance your abilities as a leader. This book is one of those occasions.

When it comes to leadership in the real world, what exactly is missing? From my perspective, it is real lessons from real leaders in relatable language. Specifically, it is the lessons that are the easiest to learn because they look you in the eye and speak directly to you in a language you can absolutely understand. This is a book, written by a real leader, for those who want to learn pragmatic lessons, grow their business, and have fun during the journey. You'll find lessons about decision making, building a strong team, and crafting strategy, along with many other crucial business turning points. This is the stuff that everyone thinks CEOs magically understand, but in reality took years, even decades, to truly acknowledge and learn.

I am one of those leaders who has spent enough time in the trenches, and in the leadership roles, to help make a difference in your life. As a former business executive with 25 years in management, I led teams as large as 7,000, was CEO of several companies, and have served on more than ten boards of directors. I did a lot of good work as part of those teams, but I also made a lot of mistakes. Like me, you may have discovered that mistakes offer great growth opportunities, as long as you take the time to reflect and directly learn from them. The reality is that if you are not making mistakes, you are not trying hard enough!

Though I love to have fun, I take my responsibility as an advisor to business leaders very seriously. I'm not just another former executive telling war stories; there are enough of those already. For the last decade, I've worked with other CEOs and executives to lead better, profit more, build a strong and steadfast team, and sleep more soundly at night, without the need for medication.

In business, we talk a great deal about the notion of *return*: Return on investment, cash-on-cash return, return on equity, and return on invested capital. Return is an important word in our business. However, whether you're a current CEO or a sales rep that wants to be one, perhaps your most important measurement of return is your return on time.

With respect to that, my promise to you is that I'll do my best to ensure that if you invest time into this book, your return will be one of value. Even if only once, I believe this book will help you to make a better decision, or avoid a costly mistake, as a result of the lessons found within these pages. When you have finished this book, you will feel more informed, more knowledgeable, and more adept to move people from point A to point B.

I am confident that my victories and failures will offer important learning opportunities for your career. As a leader, you often feel alone. But this book can act as a companion along your journey, uplifting you and giving you the tools and resources to get the job done and make a difference in the lives of your team. As I've learned, making one good decision or avoiding one bad can be the difference between being wildly successful and tragically failing.

I want to help you succeed!

Todd Ordal

CHAPTER ONE

THE ARGUMENT FOR LEADERSHIP

B y the end of this book, I am confident you will see, in fact feel, why leadership is absolutely essential in the quest for success within a business or organization. In fact, when it comes to outpacing the competition, there may not be a more important quality than strong leadership.

Now, some organizations succeed even with poor leadership. But eventually they will find themselves in the graveyard of businesses past. It is thoughtful and caring leaders that keep your business alive and breathing. They are like oxygen—they nourish and they help you to prosper, to grow. With great leadership, the sky is the limit. Without it, your wings will inevitably be clipped.

But leadership isn't always easy. There isn't a handbook to manufacture great leaders. There is no mathematical equation or algorithm that predicts leadership success. But that doesn't mean there aren't tried and true qualities that strong leaders possess. You can get lucky as a leader. Things can fall your way. But over time, if you lack strong leadership qualities, the truth will eventually surface. While leadership is arguably the most important ingredient for success, there are other ingredients that impact the results of a business.

Timing is important in business. Hit a market on the upswing and you may be very successful, even if you have significant weaknesses in your personal life or business capabilities. You might have been born on third base, thinking you hit a triple, or you might feel like the luckiest person on the planet, but timing (even luck!) can play a big role in success.

Strategy is important in business. Identify how you will distinguish yourself from the competition and you may be very successful. Truthfully, I don't see well crafted and articulated strategy come from weak leaders very often, but I do have examples of the mercurial, self-absorbed leader who comes up with a great idea that can win the battle—though not usually the war.

Having the right team is important in business. Unless you are an entrepreneur with a small company who relies primarily on your own bag of tricks, you won't optimize the potential of your business unless you have a strong team. As Jim Collins said, you must have the right people on the bus. If you have a strong team around you, you might succeed for a short while with poor leadership capabilities, but talented people like to work for talented leaders, so your situation is tenuous at best.

While these other factors are worth noting, the thread that ties timing, strategy and teams together is leadership. Whether you are talking about business, a church, the military or your local elementary school, leadership really matters. You can look to your own experience in those institutions and see what a difference a talented leader makes.

Great leaders, however, can fail: Nobody bats 1,000 in the business world. If their timing is bad, their strategy incorrect, or their team weak, they probably won't get far. There are many examples of leaders who have succeeded in one environment and failed in others. Smart business is the business of playing the odds, and the odds are that without a strong leader, the business will not succeed.

I have been fortunate to work with some great leaders, and over the years have identified that they all had some common capabilities. While they all had aptitude for business and were intelligent, they all learned these common capabilities somewhere in their career.

I'd like to share those capabilities with you and give you some tools to build or enhance your leadership style. Work on them and I guarantee that you'll be a better leader. We will focus on teams, techniques and tools in following chapters, but in this first chapter, it really is all about you! So with that said, let's take some time to discuss what I believe to be the seven mantras of successful leadership.

As an overview, these include:

- *Mantra # 1: Successful Leaders are Not Nice!*
- *Mantra # 2: Visibility and Volume: Great Leaders are Seen and Heard*
- *Mantra # 3: Effective Leaders Embrace Conflict to Create Change*
- *Mantra # 4: Fantastic Leaders Value Heart And Strength*
- *Mantra # 5: IQ $\neq$ EQ*
- *Mantra # 6: Ask a Great Question Today!*
- *Mantra # 7: Only You Can Prevent Forest Fires*

Below we will discuss each of these winning mantras that, if implemented into your leadership style, will absolutely move you in the direction of greater success and achievement as a team-builder and team-leader.

Mantra # 1: *Successful Executives Are Not Nice!*

From the minute we engage with other humans (and even pets!) our parents tell us, "Be nice!" This is intended to be a catchall for eliminating behaviors like hitting, screaming, crying, or anything that makes the other people in the sandbox feel bad.

As we get older, we're rewarded for being nice. When my kids were in elementary school, their teachers frequently complimented them for being nice, as in, "He hasn't turned in any of his homework and has failed the past three tests, but he's such a nice boy!" Nice is a hat hanger, a fall back sort of position when all else fails. But when it comes to the business of leadership, you are going to quickly see that nice isn't always the best way to carry yourself.

As adults, we continue to be rewarded for being nice. My wife is nice. When someone knocks on the door trying to sell magazine subscriptions or cookies, or even trim our trees, she happily has a meaningful conversation with whoever interrupted dinnertime. Even when she says "no," she says it nicely and only after a detailed explanation as to why she doesn't need the trees trimmed or another subscription to a magazine filled mostly with ads.

Practically, there isn't much harm in this behavior. The worst-case scenario is a nominal loss of time and too many Girl Scout cookies in the pantry. However, when we lead and manage others, being nice isn't always the most effective approach.

There's a substantial difference between being nice and being kind. Nice is born out of fear, and kind is born out of love. The fear of not being liked, or fear of conflict, prevents us from speaking the truth. But if we are kind, we will overcome that fear. Most of the time, you are willing to tell someone you love that they are making a big mistake, even at the risk of offending them or hurting their feelings.

My wife doesn't want to offend the salesperson, so she sacrifices her time to alleviate any possible rejection on the salesperson's part. She is just really nice. However, the key resource that salesperson has is time. By being nice, my wife is unintentionally reducing the salesperson's productivity and in essence, future earnings. My wife's niceness is robbing the guy blind.

What my wife doesn't realize is that spending inordinate amounts of time with people who you'll eventually tell "no thanks" is not kind. Heck, it might even be pretty mean. Instead, a kind response might be: "I'm not interested and don't want you to waste your time because I'm not purchasing anything." It may be blunt, but it the kindest and most effective response.

When my two daughters were still living at home, I could count on them to be kind and tell me that I looked like a nerd when I put on some outdated clothes. Their honesty (even if it hurt my feelings in the immediacy) saved me piles of embarrassment over the long haul. And I truly appreciated that honesty. It was not always nice, but it certainly came from the heart, and maybe a strong desire to be seen with a fashionable father.

I also appreciate it when someone tells me I look foolish with a piece of spinach in my teeth, rather than just ignore the situation because they don't want to embarrass me or seem rude. Sometimes being kind means risking offense.

Now let's apply this nice versus kind behavior to the work environment. Nice managers will always find something to compliment. Kind managers will tell you what you need to know to succeed, even when the message is that your current practices are screwing things up. Nice leaders don't want anyone to feel bad, but when they stand in the middle of the road, they end up getting hit by traffic going both ways.

Not only do they fail to protect people's feelings, they end up losing a lot more than just the smile on their face.

Real Lesson: The world is full of nice people, but only the kind ones are effective advisors and executives.

Kind leaders know that leaving weak people on the team means it won't succeed as quickly or as well. The result will be detrimental to the entire team, and eventually, the leader.

Nice leaders don't enforce the rules if someone will get upset, because to change behavior would require uncomfortable conversations. They don't challenge the simple things like tardy behavior, and as a result, work production is weak.

Kind leaders know that pushing people to be better, pointing out weaknesses and strengths, and having difficult conversations as soon as they are needed leads to much more success and, ironically, makes most people happier in the long run. They don't worry so much about the poor performers who can't handle kind and assertive conversations. They kindly escort them out of the company and allow them to find another place to settle—a nice place. It creates a successful atmosphere for everyone because they know you care, but will not be taken advantage of.

In my work as an adviser to senior executives, I've often seen nice behavior cause tremendous problems. Avoiding conflict, allowing weak people to drag others down, being nice to vendors who don't deliver, and telling board members and senior executives what they want to hear rather than the unvarnished truth are just a few examples of extremely dangerous behaviors. In fact, it destroys value, hampers employment and creates weak performers. In the end, being nice is not kind.

Is your organization nice or kind? Here are some diagnostic questions:

1. Do people speak their minds or hold back because of what others will think?
2. Do weak performers stay employed even though they add no value?
3. If you're the CEO, do you hear about problems before they're catastrophes, or is everything just fine until the doo-doo hits the fan?
4. According to performance reviews, is your company like Garrison Keillor's Lake Wobegon, where everyone is above average?
5. Have you ever reorganized a department to "work around" an ineffective person?
6. Is healthy conflict not only allowed, but also encouraged?

Mantra # 2: *Visibility and Volume:*
Great Leaders are Seen and Heard

Most of us involved in organized religion follow and pray to a god that we cannot see and hear with our normal senses, though we most always have a physical representation of our god and the written word. However, in an organizational setting, asking people to follow you when they cannot see you and cannot hear you is downright crazy. While you might send out a picture of yourself to be placed in the lunchroom, and even ask employees to gaze into your eyes while they listen to your voicemails or read your tweets, great leadership takes a whole lot more than just being a pretty face on the wall.

I once ran a large, geographically dispersed division that had just hired a new CEO. In our first substantial meeting, he asked me if he could see my communication plan. My what? People actually have written communication plans? I swallowed my pride and told him that I had communication practices, but no written plan. He gave me a couple of days to put one together, and it was a great exercise. I now serve on a public company's board that has very detailed communication plans for both internal and external messages with specific dates, events, communication medium, and spokespersons. They are clear, visible, and apparent for all to see and hear.

CEOs often fall into the trap of believing that if they say something once, or send out a memo, it will happen; like Captain Picard of Star Trek's Enterprise when he said, "Make it so!" in his deep baritone voice. Sorry, but that dog don't hunt! It takes so much more.

If a CEO has one key role, it is the keeper of the strategy—but more on that later. For our purposes here, just know that in order to execute that strategy, leaders must be visible and they must be excellent communicators. That doesn't mean that you must have a voice like Nat King Cole, the charisma of Bill Clinton, or the word choice of Ernest Hemmingway. However, it does mean that you must maintain the ability to deliver compelling messages of strategic importance and carry the persistence to stay on task and in the trenches.

Think of the great leaders that you admire. They all have different styles. Some may be downright goofy, but they probably all have the ability to get the message across in a way that galvanizes action. Ronald Reagan, Steve Jobs, Margaret Thatcher, Jack Welch, Bill Clinton, and Martin Luther King are as different as night and day, but they are all leader's who had the ability to get people to follow them through their use of language and their ability to be both seen and heard.

But how? My opinion is that great leaders are both seen and heard through the manner in which they communicate. These communication skills are fundamental, if not imperative, to the message you send and the medium through which you send it. If we are going to build great leaders, we are going to have to first create fantastic communicators. Through speech, writing, and any other way leaders offer the "message," the goal has got to be to make it clear, precise, strategized, and fundamentally aligned with the company's purpose.

Communication skills can be learned. If you are going to be an effective leader, communicating in a compelling fashion should be near the top of your list for personal development. The content (i.e. vision and strategy) is critical as well, or you'll be—as they say in Texas—all hat and no cattle. To state the obvious, if you do not have the ability to get people to follow you, you'll never lead effectively. And if your followers don't know what you want, they won't know in which direction to travel.

Extemporaneous speaking is a valuable skill, but don't kid yourself; most great communicators spend lots of time preparing. If you think long and hard about what you are trying to communicate, you'll be able to respond quickly when necessary. What slows us down is not being mentally prepared.

There are a multitude of public speaking classes available and you can develop your vocabulary through some hard work. Likewise, writing can be taught as well. No excuses here!

Position authority (e.g. the title "CEO") will only get you to the starting line. A title without a team is like a rancher with no animals. Unless you own the majority of the stock of a company, your title only confers the role you seek to play. If you want to be a real leader, you must be able to answer three simple, but not easy, questions: Where are we going? What will we do to get there? How will we do it? Once you answer these questions, you must be able to clearly and effectively communicate them to your team.

Real Lesson: If you don't communicate effectively, get some training and put some effort into it! You must be visible (which in today's world can involve technology), you must stay on message, and you must say it forcefully.

Mantra # 3: *Effective Leaders*
Embrace Conflict to Create Change

Conflict is one of the topics with which CEOs most often struggle. Unfortunately, the prevalent mindset is that you should minimize it. That is wrong—you should *optimize* it. Let me explain.

I recently gathered a group of executives together to discuss organizational conflict. Early in the conversation, I asked them to rate the level of conflict in their organization on a specific scale. On one end of the continuum was a high level of conflict both in frequency and veracity, with personal attacks as commonplace. On the other end of the scale was conflict avoidance where everyone was "nice," but important issues were completely ignored. In the middle was optimal conflict, where people were comfortable speaking their mind, differing opinions were explored with focus on the issue rather than individuals, and the arguments were evidence based. Most every executive rated their organization as being firmly on the conflict avoidance side of the scale.

If there is too much conflict in your organization, you will not have productive conversations. People will worry more about winning the argument than moving the business ahead. In extreme situations—usually the result of a highly combative CEO—there are two possible scenarios. The first is the company is full of aggressive people who care much more about their personal gain than the success of the team. The second scenario is that the company chews through talented people who won't allow the abuse, and is therefore left with very weak players. If there is too little conflict, the end result is the same: business suffers. Good ideas are not surfaced and silly behavior is tolerated because no one wants to hurt feelings.

Organizations with too much conflict or too little conflict often have the following characteristics:

- Confusing organizational design and/or authority limits
- Objectives, strategy and vision not clear
- Values not clearly stated
- Lack of trust
- Unwillingness to hold others accountable
- Hallway reversals allowed (lack of commitment)
- Some bad apples on the team
- CEO not modeling the correct behavior
- Misaligned rewards

I once facilitated a meeting with the top 30 people of a large organization. They were conflict averse and wanted to move towards the sweet spot on the conflict scale. One executive described a meeting that he recently attended with his colleagues in the room as a complete waste of time. The other executives all nodded their heads in agreement. Imagine the top 30 people in a large firm spending hours in a non-productive meeting and remaining silent for fear of hurt feelings. Now imagine that happening a few times month! What are the hard costs (salaries and benefits) and the opportunity costs of that continued behavior?

The truth is you'd be surprised how often your co-workers and team members are thinking the same thing as you. And if someone just embraced a little bit of conflict, everyone would be better for it.

Here is an assessment tool that you can use with your team to identify the level of healthy conflict in your organization. You can use it in two different ways:

1. After a meeting, ask the participants to rate the meeting on this scale.
2. Ask your team members to rate the typical interactions within the organization.

Conflict Measurement Tool	
– 4 – 3 – 2 – 1 Optimal + 1 + 2 + 3 + 4	
–4	Complete avoidance of conflict even if the issue is critical. Parties unwilling to engage. No resolution possible. Fosters increased lack of trust and respect.
–3	Tentative discussion of what should be a significant issue. Unlikely that issue is moving forward. No resolution. Parties have little trust in each other.
–2	Issue raised but non-assertive communication. May be goal oriented, but fear of stepping on others' toes reduces the effectiveness of the conversation. Parties may not be familiar or have a history of ineffective communication.
–1	Goal focused. Respectful but overly polite (nice) conversation. Issue moved forward, but not all elements explored fully.
Desired State. Assertive communication. Goal focused. Mostly respectful communication. All voices heard. May still be strong discussions, but tough issues are moved forward.	
+1	Tense but goal focused. Participants with low tolerance for conflict may still be uncomfortable. Some statements become personal but are corrected.
+2	Uncomfortable. Slight positive results are possible (e.g. goal oriented actions or statements). Still more goal oriented than personal.
+3	Very uncomfortable. Not goal oriented. Statements are more personal than goal oriented. Situation is salvageable if parties regain control.
+4	Very heated discussion. Voices raised and loss of control by participants. Personal attacks. No positive results. Often exacerbates the problem. Situation not salvageable without significant intervention, probably by a 3rd party.

You'll notice—if you make use of this assessment tool—that people have different levels of comfort with conflict. Some of us were raised in homes where conflict was taboo. For instance, I grew up in the Midwest in a community that was primarily Scandinavian in heritage, and conflict was not valued. Overall, people were "nice." They also ate lutefisk (cod soaked in lye) and potato dumplings, which may explain the lack of fire in their bellies. However, some of you grew up in other regions in the country with families who embraced a culture of frequent conflict.

As the leader of the organization, conflict is one of the "levers" available to you in your quest to craft a healthy culture. Start by asking yourself these questions:

- What is your comfort level with conflict?
- Does it feel like the issues in meetings are fully explored or are there opinions and facts left out?
- Do my team members confront each other when performance is not what it should be?
- Do my team members look for feedback from others in meetings—even those with whom they disagree?
- Are people comfortable pushing back at me when they think that I'm wrong?

What do you do if you believe that you have a lack of healthy conflict in your organization? Follow these steps:

1. Establish trust (more on this later)
2. Establish clear vision/objectives
3. Minimize personal attacks
4. Maximize evidence based discussions
5. Optimize preparation for decisions

6. Encourage healthy debate
7. Insist on commitment once a decision is made

But, what if you have too much unhealthy conflict?

1. Make sure that objectives are clear
2. Don't allow personal attacks
3. Enforce agreements
4. Leaders must model and reward correct behavior

Remember, creating a culture that embraces positive conflict starts with your attitude towards conflict. If you huff and puff every time something doesn't go your way, your team will notice exactly how you handle conflict, and avoid it at all costs. But if they see a consistent and steadfast leader, they will maintain that same composure when the going gets tough. Many leaders assume that conflict is just a by-product of interaction and that it is merely a result of individual personality. I don't believe that. In my experience, you can think about conflict as a manageable tool on an organizational level. Remember, the objective is not to minimize conflict, but rather to *optimize* it!

Real Lesson: You, as CEO, must be comfortable with healthy conflict and optimize it in your company.

Mantra # 4: *Fantastic Leaders Value Heart And Strength*
CEO's are supposed to be infallible, but in reality they are human, and when they keep emotions bottled up, the consequences can be substantial. Effective executives are not only courageous and forceful, but they are also vulnerable and demonstrate that they have big hearts. They are always confident, but not always certain. In fact, the most fantastic leaders in the world care deeply for those that they lead. They trade open door policies for open ear practices, always willing to listen

to, and support their team. They find time to dive into the lives of their colleagues, and are willing to build relationships based on a genuine and authentic care for team member's personal and professional concerns.

They do so through the mutual exchange of feelings, information, and emotions. Author Patrick Lencioni calls this type of vulnerability "getting naked," and correctly asserts that this must start at the top, or it will not happen at all. CEO's often believe that they have to have all of the answers, and constantly appear to be strong. This mindset puts them into a very uncomfortable box—one that literally is constraining and problematic.

I once had a coaching meeting with a talented but "boxed in" CEO. I asked him if he felt as if he had to have all of the answers. It was clear he felt that he had to solve every problem within the business. He couldn't ever appear weak or exposed, and always had to show a strong front, even when he felt inner doubt and self-worth. He was not relying on his team, and he was boxing himself in. He needed help, but didn't know how to show his vulnerability and just ask.

There has been a great deal of press in the last few decades about the ineffectiveness of "top down" management. Most of this, of course, was spewed forth by people who never had accountability for an organization. Too many people internalized this criticism and foolishly believed that they could abdicate their position in the name of collaboration. This is naive! Culture and strategy must be driven from the top down. And it must start by being a human being with human feelings.

Don't kid yourself! If you are the CEO, you are accountable. You are the top dog, not the top earthworm. You do not, however, have to have all of the answers or always appear as a man (or woman) made of steel. You can be vulnerable in front of your people and even your customers. In fact, that vulnerability welcomes in other opinions and is the quickest way to gain the trust of your team. You appear to be relatable, trustworthy, and real.

President John Adams said, "If there is one central truth to be collected from the history of all ages, it is this: that the people's rights and liberties, and the democratical (sic) mixture in a constitution, can never be preserved without a strong executive."

And so it is with business.

Strong executives may be collaborative, but they're decisive. They may be kind, but they don't avoid tough decisions. They likely understand and support pushing decisions to the lowest effective level, but they insist on great execution at that level. They don't need to control all the details, but they insist on high performance.

I've had the great fortune of working with numerous strong executives, and some weak ones. Weak executives foster weak organizations, but strong executives don't necessarily foster strong organizations. Strength—that is, power, decisiveness, forcefulness, fearlessness and confidence—isn't enough, but it's a darn good start. Couple strength with passion, intelligence, and vulnerability, and you have the building blocks of successful leadership. Without vulnerability, a strong leader simply becomes a tyrant.

We all know and love numerous people who are indecisive, lack force and confidence, and have many fears. It's unlikely, however, that those people are successful in executive roles. They may be brilliant artists, designers, engineers, scientists, caregivers or teachers, but they shouldn't be in leadership roles.

I've seen emotionally intelligent, passionate, and intellectually capable people in senior leadership roles crumble because they weren't strong enough. They weren't strong enough to stand up to their board when asked to do ridiculous things, to fire people who needed to be fired, to not need everyone to love them, or to say, "follow me" in a way that people responded to. Remain strong enough to be vulnerable, admit mistakes, and ask for help. And remember, your heart is the most important door to constantly leave open.

Real Lesson: You can learn to be strong, as long as you are not afraid to show vulnerability and ask for help. Strength and vulnerability are not mutually exclusive!

Mantra # 5: *IQ ≠ EQ*

Years ago, my Vice President of Sales, Sam, wanted to make an unusual hire in a sales management position and asked me to interview the candidate to get my feedback. In preparation for meeting the candidate, I asked Sam about his background and he told me that he was a "rocket scientist." "O.K., so he's smart. I expected that," I said, "but what is he doing for a living?" "He's a *rocket scientist!* He builds rockets," said Sam. While it was great that he had an enormous IQ (much bigger than mine), it was clear he did not possess the social or leadership skills necessary for the position.

It's not good enough to be smart. That may get you into a leadership role, but it is emotional intelligence (often abbreviated "EQ" or "EI") that will allow you to succeed. As an executive, there are some things that you should know about emotional intelligence.

Here are three of the most important:

1. You can measure it.
2. You can improve it.
3. You are more likely to get fired for lack of EQ than IQ!

If the last point didn't get your attention, it really might be an IQ issue! Differing models use different language, but for our purposes, let's stick with the basics from Daniel Goleman's model and talk about self-awareness, self-management, social-awareness and social skill.

Self-awareness means that you have a solid understanding of what you are good at and the areas where you need to improve. If someone were to ask all of those who engage with you to describe your style, personality, and habits, these should mirror your own description. We are all breathing our own exhaust to some degree, but it is very important that the image you have of yourself is not significantly different than the image others have of you.

Some tools to increase self-awareness include:

- Feedback from trusted sources. This means that they must a) see you in your work setting (preferably social setting as well), and b) be willing to speak the truth.
- 360-degree feedback tools can be very helpful. However, they must be administered appropriately or the data is garbage. Never forget—when you are at the top of the heap, most people want to please you and many are fearful to tell you the truth!
- Learn to watch how people respond to you when you are not in a superior-subordinate relationship (e.g. when you are with peers, friends, or at the shopping mall).

Self-management means that you can take your self-awareness and do something with it. It means that you don't fly off the handle frequently. It means that you are able to remain calm even when you are fearful. It means that you can delay gratification and can adjust to fluid situations. This can all be enhanced with practice and coaching. Once again, if you have challenges in this area, it is imperative to have someone who can help you through this, someone who will be a truth-talker.

Social awareness means that you are able to understand how others are feeling. It means that you are able to understand social clues like facial expressions, language, and posture. It means that you can anticipate how people will act and feel in many situations. Great sales people (not the show-up-and-throw-up variety!) often have a high level of social awareness. As a CEO, you are often selling your ideas, and the manner in which you communicate them is critical.

Social skill means that you know what to do with your awareness of others. The leader who relies on position authority—"I'm the CEO, damn it!"—rather than the authority that comes from social skill is rarely successful in the long-term. With social skill you can adjust your style to make people want to listen to you. You can inspire and influence others. You know how to make friends. You know how to negotiate. You understand the power of questions rather than making pronouncements. This is the backbone for EQ.

IQ is important, especially if you are a rocket-scientist. But to be a great leader, IQ plays a significantly smaller role than your ability to communicate, implement strategy, and lead a team all the way to the promised land of success.

Real Lesson: Have others who know you well (and who will speak the truth!) help identify your level of self-awareness and social-awareness. If you are lacking, create an action plan to improve. Pick up a copy of Daniel Goleman's book, *Emotional Intelligence,* if you'd like a better understanding of this mantra.

Mantra # 6: *Ask a Great Question Today!*

Isador Rabi, a recipient of the Nobel prize for physics, gives credit to his mother for helping him become a scientist. He said that when he was a child, his friends' mothers would ask their children when returning from school, "Did you learn anything today?" Yet his mother would ask, "Did you ask a good question today?"

I recall a specific situation where a CEO asked a very tough and strategic question during a board meeting. This large board, full of very bright people, spent quite some time crafting well-articulated answers to the posed question. After about thirty minutes of debate, a particularly smart fellow identified that the question was not the right question. He reframed the issue with a much better question, which led to a much different conversation. The actual situation had not changed, but the fact that the board was now focused with the right lens made all the difference in the world.

Those of you who are basketball fans know that sometimes an outgunned team can win the game by slowing it down, controlling the pace, and thereby playing a more surgical game. Run and gun doesn't always win the day. As a business leader, sometimes you need to slow the game down and be more thoughtful in your approach. It is very easy for an individual or a team to respond to a question, and then they are off to the races—down the wrong road!

Here are some examples of reframing questions:

- Rather than asking, "How should we grow our European market?" you might ask, "Where will we receive the best return on our investment in growth?"
- Rather than asking, "How should we solve this problem?" you might ask, "Is this problem large enough to allocate resources to solve?"
- Rather than asking, "Should we be focused on top-line or bottom-line growth next year?" you might ask, "How can we grow our top line next year without compromising our margins?"

Get the idea? Framing questions effectively is one of the most valuable skills you can develop as an executive! Take the time to think before you speak and always understand the type of answer you are seeking, so you can better tailor the question.

Real Lesson: Leaders should focus more on asking the right questions rather than giving the right answers. The wrong question, answered accurately, always produces the wrong answer for the situation at hand. You can practice this by asking, "How else could we look at this issue?" Another exercise is to spend a few days keeping track of the number of questions that you ask of others, and the amount of time you spend listening vs. talking. You might be surprised.

Mantra # 7: *Only You Can Prevent Forest Fires*

It is dangerous for a leader to become a full-time firefighter. Perhaps you saw the movie "Backdraft," where Robert De Niro plays an arson investigator? De Niro's character discovers that the mystery antagonist and arsonist is actually a fireman. In the real world, this is perhaps a rarity. But in business, some leaders love to start fires because the adrenaline rush of coming to the rescue is addictive.

Dwight Eisenhower said, "In preparing for battle I have always found that plans are useless, but planning is indispensable." You clearly can't plan for every contingency in a fast-paced business, but if your vision and strategy are clear, you can avoid many of the fires. And when the unavoidable occurs, you are ready to take action without hesitation. In the immortal words of Smokey the Bear, "Only you can prevent forest fires."

While you should avoid becoming a full-time firefighter, as a leader, you cannot run from fires. In fact, you have to be ready to run right into them. You must have courage.

My youngest son was a Marine and served in Iraq. He happened to be in Fallujah and saw some awful things. He also had many great experiences and was proud to serve our country. He told me that as he was leaving his outpost to return to the United States, an elder in the local community said to him, "We run from trouble, but you crazy Marines, you run right into it!"

"What makes a king out of a slave? Courage! What makes the flag on the mast to wave? Courage! What makes the elephant charge his

tusk in the misty mist or the dusky dusk? What makes the muskrat guard his musk? Courage! What makes the sphinx the seventh wonder? Courage! What makes the dawn come up like thunder? Courage! What makes the Hottentot so hot? Courage! What have they got that I ain't got? Courage!"

—The Cowardly Lion from the "Wizard of Oz"

Courage might be defined as acting in the face of danger without fear, or perhaps it's ignoring your fear to do what's necessary and get the job done. Although having courage alone isn't sufficient to succeed as a leader, it certainly gets you into the conversation.

Reed Hastings, the CEO of Netflix, took the extremely unpopular decision to radically change his business model several years ago at the risk of upsetting many customers. His courageous decision paid off. Likewise, Steve Jobs famously and courageously scrapped many products to focus on a few great ones when he returned to save Apple after it fell into disrepute. He knew that if the company was going to be successful, he needed to focus his resources rather than have a basket full of mediocre products.

On the other hand, weak leaders don't have the chutzpah, passion or confidence to take courageous action. They continue to eat lavish dinners in the captain's quarters as the ship takes on water. Sunny skies and calm seas? They look great in their dressed up uniform with their hand on the wheel. But when storms break out, their true mettle is tested.

Deciding which color to paint the conference room doesn't require courage. Giving rah-rah speeches about needing customer service, innovation or ethical behavior doesn't warrant much courage. Flying around in the company jet to slap backs or attend golf tournaments doesn't demand courage. As Epicurus said, *"You don't develop courage by being happy in your relationships every day. You develop it by surviving difficult times and challenging adversity."*

Hiring a senior person who'll stir things up requires courage. Making a strategic choice to abandon large markets or customer groups necessitates courage. Firing loved team members who don't have what you need to get to the next level demands courage. Looking at the future and deciding that your business model needs dramatic change requires courage. Risking your job and your position to make a change you believe in takes a lot of courage. Great leaders maintain that courage, along with the seven mantras mentioned above. These pillars help to shape great leaders and maintain crystal-clear focus in otherwise muddied waters.

Real Lesson: Real leaders do not run from trouble, nor do they become full-time firefighters. They are courageous and know that they must occasionally fail in order to achieve the greatest amount of success. What are you avoiding right now that needs to be dealt with?

This chapter contains the foundation for a successful leadership career. These mantras need to become part of your daily routine. We will explore some of them in even more depth as we progress further into the book. Feel free to return to this chapter often for a refresher on these building blocks.

Chapter Review:

Listen Up: I'm hopeful that much of what you read above resonated with you, but it is imperative that you immediately pick one mantra to work on—yes, right now! Identify two or three activities to support that mantra and get them on your calendar. It only takes a few minutes to make a singular change. If you dedicate time to just one change a day, the annual return on your investment will be substantial.

Quick Wins: Share these mantras with three trusted colleagues who are in a position to observe you in your leadership role. Get their feedback on your performance level in these areas to see how you can improve on each one.

<u>Graduate Work:</u> Create your own annual personal development plan from these mantras. Make sure that you cement behavioral changes in one area before you tackle another one. By the end of the year, you—and others—will see significant improvement!

CHAPTER TWO

WHEN THE DOG CATCHES THE CAR, WHAT DOES HE DO?

Most of the time, the chase is where the real journey lies. But what happens when we obtain that which we are chasing? When it comes to leadership, signing on the dotted line is the easy part. It is the journey that begins *after* you accept the position that really counts. Your legacy, your imprint, and your impact begin once you settle in in your new office.

Think strategically. Lead from the front. Remove obstacles. Wander around.

While there are lots of exhortations on how to lead once you are empaneled in your new position, they are not necessarily one-size fits all. So, what do you actually do? How do you spend your time and with whom? What steps can you take to become the best possible leader for your team?

These are just some of the questions that, together, we will work to address and answer because, in reality, these are the answers that make the difference in the environment and culture of leadership. These are the answers that provide you the necessary tools to simultaneously develop your team and your leadership abilities.

I'd like to frame and then discuss the *"What do I do?"* question before we jump into the answers and actual steps you can take to develop as a leader. Years ago, I was hired to be CEO of a midsize company. Although I had been president of a 7,000-person division and served on the board of several organizations, this was my first stint as a CEO.

While my first week on the job afforded me the opportunity to meet everyone and even fight some unexpected raging fires, I vividly remember walking into my office on the first day of the second week and thinking to myself, "What exactly is it that I am suppose to *do* here?" I had chased after the car, latched onto the bumper, and was travelling at a high rate of speed, unsure as to what I was supposed to do!

This is a feeling often all too familiar to newly anointed leaders. They catch the car, but then what? I started by using the most valuable tool that I know of in business—the question. Through asking specific and thoughtful questions, you will find the opportunity to secure an enormously helpful wealth of knowledge regarding the inner-workings and inner-feelings of your team and your company.

Picking your questions is just as important as picking your team members. Asking the right questions will offer you valuable information and insight so you can optimize your ability to do your job and accomplish your goals.

Over my years and experience in the leadership world, I have worked hard to consider the most impactful type of questions. With that said, here are the three framing questions that I used to better understand what I should be doing. I believe that they will be helpful for any CEO—seasoned or new to the role—to discover how it is that he or she can succeed and best benefit the organization. The answers to these questions will provide the context for your work as the most senior leader of the organization. They are:

1. What are the most important levers in our business and how can I best focus upon them?
2. How can I best leverage my strengths and either improve or minimize my weaknesses?
3. What is it that only I can do that will bring value to the organization?

What do I need to know, and know how to do? If you have successfully led an organization for some time, the answers to these framing questions might fly out of your mouth. If they don't, please do not despair, you are in the right place. Together we will help you find these answers. If you are new to an organization, or if your environment (internal or external) has recently changed, you'll recognize that the answers to these questions are not static.

Before you read any further—whether you are a grizzled veteran or have been recently promoted—I'd like you to sit down right now and try to write out the answers to those questions. The truth is that at some point it will be the answers to these questions that will make or break your success as a leader. If you struggle with your answers, the rest of the book will help.

Asking these questions and securing the answers are integral parts to the success of any leader. Ask the wrong questions and you will not only get the wrong answers, but you will likely waste your most important resource—time. As a leader, you'll find a direct correlation between how you spend your time and the success of the organization you lead. That being said, I want to talk about this currency that we are all forced to use—either wisely or foolishly.

Time: Your Most Precious Resource

As Albert Einstein said, *"The only reason for time is so that everything doesn't happen at once."* How much time you apply to work is up to you. Whether you are a 65-hour a week kind of guy, or you are talented enough to balance work and home life more effectively, we are all blessed with the same number of potential work hours in a week. Thus, it is important to remain conscious about how you make choices with your time based upon your values, your personal needs, the needs of those you care about, and the needs of the business that you lead.

Most CEOs that I have coached remain challenged by balancing time at work with personal and family time. If this were an easy task to accomplish, you wouldn't get paid the big bucks! I don't have a magic bullet for you, but I would encourage you to appreciate that the time conundrum is a struggle that we all have. Shut your door, unplug your phone, and reflect. You'll need to make compromises, so I encourage you to take the long-term view and understand that you can make adjustments as your circumstances change. Time is inflexible, but how you use your time is a choice.

Getting a *Return* on Your Time

If you are reading this book, you likely have a good deal of discretion as to how you spend your time. It's unlikely that someone forced you to read this. You decided that at this moment, this is what you should do. You decided to invest your time into the resources and tools this book will provide.

The $59 time-management seminar I went to 30 years ago started off with this statement: "Regardless of who you are, we all have 24 hours in our day." I don't recall anyone jumping up to argue. In fact, it may have been the only thing we all agreed upon. This obvious point still holds true today. However, we now have hundreds of cable channels, social media opportunities, cell phones, email, YouTube, and many more distractions with which to contend. I watched "The Jetsons" as a kid and thought about how cool it would be to have Rosie the robot maid with all of those gadgets so I'd have more free time. I stopped holding my breath a long time ago.

I've worked with many leaders and often had conversations with them about how to best spend their time. As a result, I came up with *Seven Timely Tips for Increasing Return on Time*. These tips will help you trim the fat and analyze where the time goes, so you can better evaluate where you can optimize your time and prevent the waste of this valuable resource.

1. **Clarify your values.** A great place to start taking control of your time is by identifying your values and then determining whether the activities and time you're investing (or squandering) are consistent with these values.

2. **Plan**. If you don't plan, how can you know what's most important? If an activity doesn't take you closer to your long-term objectives, do you need to do it, or did you get sidetracked? (It's OK to look at shiny new things occasionally.)

3. **Be assertive**. You don't need to have a relationship with everybody who rings your doorbell or calls you on the phone. Trying to be nice to everyone (see chapter one) prevents you from doing what you should be doing. A talented client who's CEO of a large company recently said, "I don't want to be seen as a jerk, but I just can't go to lunch with everyone who asks." Some will see him as a jerk, but he's right.

4. **Use "comparative advantage" to your advantage.** (If you aren't familiar with the economics term "comparative advantage,"

look it up. I swear it'll be a good use of your time.) If you love to mow the lawn, great! If not, get someone who's faster and then find a better outlet for your time. I had a client who swore he could do everything better than all of his employees. He probably could, but, in trying to do so, he was miserable and couldn't grow his business.

5. **Define wealth in terms of well-being, not just money.** This causes you to think differently about your activities and what has value. The guy I referenced in bullet point four was financially wealthy, but couldn't take a vacation even though he could afford to buy a jet to do so! I'm writing this on a Monday. I'm skiing tomorrow because there's supposed to be a foot of new snow. (Admittedly, it might be a late night tonight!) Tomorrow, I'll be wealthier than the guy with the pile of money.

6. **Recognize that longer is not better.** Pretend you're hiring me as a consultant to help you solve a large problem. It's going to take six months and require a $250,000 investment, but it will bring in $10 million in new revenue. Wait ... I just found a way to do it in five minutes. Does this have more or less value to you? Longer is not better; it's just longer.

7. **Relax.** Nobody gets this right all the time. Just course-correct frequently.

The further up in the organization that you are, the more valuable to the organization your time will be. Unfortunately, you also have many people and projects competing for your time and attention.

You have a good deal of latitude on how you spend your time, and at the end of the day, time is your most valuable resource. A local radio personality was reviewing a movie some time ago and he said, "That movie was so bad, I didn't want my $10 back, I wanted the three hours of my life back!" No matter what you do, time is a valuable resource.

Real Lesson: It is what you *do* as a leader that will define you. Your calendar must reflect what you want to do. How you use your time will create the story of your success or failure.

The Five Levers of Success

You've now created a framework for what is important in your business by answering the three key framing questions at the beginning of the chapter. You have also thought about time as your most valuable resource. Now we get to the "what?"

If leading was as easy as pulling levers up and down to create change and develop your team, we'd all be out of a job. A trained monkey could do that. The truth is that there are levers to pull, but you also have to build the machine that responds. Greek philosopher Archimedes said, "Give me a place to stand and with a lever I will move the whole world."

By using your time wisely and implementing the structure your business so desperately requires, you'll begin to plot the course to burn a path that leaves a lasting and positive imprint on your team and your business. With that said, let's focus on the important levers that we'd all like to have in place. What follows are what I call *The Five Levers of Success* for a senior leader.

They are:

1. Planning vs. Responding
2. Deeply understanding your customers
3. Look Under The Hood—Your Employees and Partners
4. Winning or Losing? Financial Performance
5. Personal development

For each of these levers, I have created questions that I believe you should ask yourself weekly. Good practice is to do this

Sunday night before the opening bell on Monday morning, but you might block out time on your calendar to do this first thing on Monday.

Lever 1: *Planning vs. Responding*

One of my best clients—a very successful CEO—has a reminder stuck to his computer screen that says:

1. Have you talked to the board today?
2. Have you reviewed the numbers today?
3. Have you walked the hallways today?
4. Have you talked to a customer today?
5. Did you read today?
6. Did you think about the future today?

While the questions may change based upon his priorities, these questions serve him very well and help to maintain his focus and keep him on a purposeful and meaningful track. It is these questions that allows this CEO to plan for what's to come. Don't overthink this. I've had clients look for the perfect planning tool or process, all the while missing out on the big picture. A pen and notepad are good enough! This is about success, not perfection.

Think about that morning when you walk into the office and immediately begin your day by putting out fires. Before you know it, you look up, buried by emergency after emergency, and find it to be after 5:00PM. This can happen when you are in response mode all day. You feel like you put in a hard day's work, but you accomplished very little over the course of the day. This is the rub when you are constantly responding instead of planning. You have much to accomplish, but don't feel like you've really optimized your time. By planning, you allow yourself to optimize your productiveness.

There is no perfect day in the C-suite. In fact there are no two days alike. You need to start with a plan. However, as former boxer Mike Tyson said, "Everyone has a plan until they get punched in the mouth!" so you need to be able to deal with ambiguity and learn how to dance as well.

Real Lesson: Maintain a plan. It needs to be in writing because we too often fool ourselves or lose sight of our priorities when they are not on paper. Create your own list of questions to answer daily or weekly.

Lever 2: *Deeply Understanding Your Customers*

Only when you fully and completely understand your customers, can you optimize and create a service or product with which they can identify and feel as if they need. It is that evaluation and analysis that so many companies miss. And the worst part is that it just takes a little bit of time and energy to reach this goal. Start with questions like:

1. Why are our customers buying from us vs. our competitors?
2. Are they happy with what they are getting?
3. What else do they want?
4. What are their greatest challenges?
5. What do they need to satisfy their customers?

I believe that the best way to answer these questions is to ask your customers directly. Don't just ask your sales and marketing teams. Here is something you must keep in mind: most everything you hear as CEO is filtered. You will not hear the real truth unless you go to the source. Your people want you to be happy. They want to impress you. They rarely will say something that could disappoint.

You need to spend some frequent time with your best or ideal customers to effectively answer these questions. By customer, I mean the decision maker, whether or not those are the senior people. Do your best to make sure that your customer visits are not dog and pony shows where you only see what others want you to see. You need real information. Schedule regular meetings to do this.

I like one-on-one visits with customers, but some companies have successfully created communities of customers —marrying information gathering with service offerings—and learned how to monetize those communities. When you can reap tangible rewards (e.g. revenue) as well as the intangible benefits of creating a sticky environment where customers come to hang out (think local pub or the virtual, digital equivalent) with each other, you've created a wonderful thing!

Real Lesson: You need to know your top customers and understand their needs. If I reviewed your calendar, how much time would be devoted to interacting with your customers?

Lever 3: *Look Under The Hood—Your Employees and Partners*

I've always felt you can learn a lot about a person by observing who he or she keeps as company. As a C-suite leader, you likely have an enormous amount of control over your employees and partners. That being said, consider the strengths and weaknesses of who you hire and those with which you partner up. Consider the following questions to determine if all is running well under the hood:

1. Are my people engaged?
2. What can I learn from them that I may not know?
3. What are they concerned about?
4. How can they best add value?
5. Are they receiving the right messages?
6. If they were CEO, what would they change?

You are only one of many people within your organization. It is with the leverage of your team that you will produce the torque from your business engine required to succeed. Is your team a rusty old V8 that only moves by adding horsepower (more people)? Or do you have a turbocharged, efficient team that produces more output per payroll dollar than your competitors?

Just like your customers, you don't want to get filtered information about your employees. Like the previously mentioned CEO with the checklist, go walk the hallways and talk to them. Take some of them to lunch. They are going to want to hear from you, but try to listen way more than you talk.

Schedule time each week to talk to a variety of people at different levels in the organization. Respect the chain of command (i.e. for goodness sake don't walk around giving orders!) and don't just look for things that are wrong. If you do, you'll create a culture that is opaque. People will hide problems faster than the squirrels in my back yard hide nuts.

If they seem clueless or are getting the wrong message, it's either your fault or that of middle management, not theirs.

When I was a division president at Kinko's, I was in charge of hundreds of stores and thousands of people. I also used to fly airplanes. Several times per year I would jump into an airplane and take a week or so to visit stores without area management along. In fact, I wouldn't even tell my assistant where I was going. That way I was assured of seeing reality. No dogs and no ponies. I'd put on an apron and work in the stores alongside our hourly coworkers, and it was the best learning experience I could have had. This was years before the T.V. show "Undercover Boss," so I wasn't smart enough to put on a costume or dye my mustache.

Real Lesson: Some of your team will not like the attention. Don't let this push you off track. If they squawk loudly, either you are too negative or they have something to hide.

It is important to also remember your hidden employees: your partners. Ask them questions like:

- What are their problems?
- Where are they winning or losing?
- How can you help them be more successful?

Some of the relationships with others outside of your formal organization are critical to your success. These might be vendors, government officials, or investors. I ran a big organization that was largely dependent upon one equipment manufacturer. I found that if I brought them closer and treated them like a partner rather than a vendor, they were much more responsive and helpful. It also made for a much more enjoyable relationship.

Make sure, however, that you *really* understand the relationship. If you cannot answer, "What is in it for them?" with certainty, or the answer is not compelling, watch out! I have seen several companies fail because they had all of their eggs in one basket—sometimes in concentration with one or a few customers, but also with one or a few key suppliers or partners (including their banker!) that suddenly took a sharp turn.

As the most senior leader in your company, you absolutely must understand all of the key stakeholder relationships.

Lever 4: *Winning or Losing? Financial Performance*

At the end of the day, it is your financial performance that will make or break your position, as well as the position of your company. As much as we would like to place value on positive vibes and good feelings, profit (or the lack thereof) will often drive many of the decisions made within the walls of an organization. That being said, we constantly have to strive to answer the question of whether we are winning or losing in the game of dollars. This begins by assessing and asking yourself the following questions:

1. How are we performing vis-à-vis the market?
2. How are we performing vis-à-vis our plan?
3. Where are we performing well and where are we missing the mark? Why?
4. Do we have adequate cash?

We will discuss financial management in detail later in the book, but you should understand where and why you are missing the mark, and also where and why you are succeeding. Allocate some time with both the winners and the laggards (e.g. products, people, market segments) and see what you can discern. These should be conversations; not rants or love fests. Write down what you learn and then meet with the right people and take action. Expand on successful practices and fix the broken ones.

The financial performance of your company is the measuring stick for how good your strategy is and how well you are executing. If you are not doing well, either the ideas that drive activity (i.e. the strategy) are wrong or there is an execution problem. (We'll address both strategy and execution in later chapters.)

A word of caution…you can drive yourself and others crazy by looking at short-term results and generalizing from them. One day's results don't make a trend. I worked with the owner of a $100 million dollar (revenue) privately held business that looked at daily cash flow—not always unreasonable—but he would allow his mood to fluctuate from despair to manic based upon yesterday's results, even though he could not identify why cash was up or down. That's not just illogical, it is silly!

I find that in most businesses, you might have a daily set of operating numbers that are important, but the financial indicators that are most often appropriate are those at the weekly level, or much longer depending upon your business model. For those of you who work in public companies, the last thing you want is the public focused on short term results!

Real Lesson: You need to know if you are winning or losing *and why!*

Lever 5: *Personal Development*

When I was a young father, I thought that by the time my kids were 18, I'd be done with parenting with the exception of sending tuition checks. (Those of you with older kids can now get back up onto your chair and quit laughing!) Little did I know that I would have to continue to learn about parenting even after I would have thought I was across the finish line!

So it is when you become a senior leader, even CEO. You probably realize that your need to keep learning is even more intense than it was early in your career because the impact of your actions are so much greater.

Here is the way I diagramed it for a coaching client:

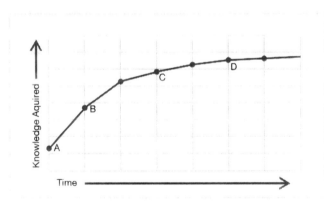

While the knowledge acquired early in your career (from A to B) is much greater than the knowledge acquired later in your career (C to D), the *impact* of that knowledge on the organization is much greater later in your career as you are influencing many more people, allocating significant assets, and making more consequential decisions.

Assuming that you know what you need to know just because you are a highly paid executive is as naïve as me assuming that I was done parenting when my kids turned 18 (Many days I still wish my mother was around to parent me and I'm close to 60!).

Acquired knowledge and skill as an executive can come from many different sources. Executive education programs at universities, mastermind groups, a seasoned executive coach, industry events, and books such as the one you are reading right now are all viable methods of staying sharp, or better yet, getting sharper! Don't just look within your firm or your industry. Expose yourself to different points of view and different sources of knowledge.

The reality is that, as a leader, you are given the gift of time. That is a borrowed gift. It is a gift lent to you by your organization. And it is one that should be cherished and respected. When you take that gift of time and use it effectively, you'll find an enormous and exciting opportunity to create real and tangible results. As a leader, time can be your friend. But it can also be the difference between retaining your job and losing it. Within this chapter, you have received some valuable tools that are literally time-tested to successfully utilize the greatest resource you have at your disposal.

Real Lesson: If you have reached the top of the organization, you have the ability to search out top quality learning opportunities, and you should!

I want to congratulate you for spending your time wisely by reading this book! As a leader, time is your greatest asset. This chapter has instructed you on how to most effectively use your time. You were also given levers that will help strengthen and grow your business, and ultimately lead you to success. Continue to focus on these as you move forward.

Chapter Review:

Listen Up: Write down the answers to the three questions at the beginning of this chapter and share them with a few confidants to see if they agree. Then create your own "Have you _____ today?" list.

Quick Wins: Take control of your calendar right now! It is the most underutilized tool in business. Your calendar needs to reflect your priorities. It should be liberating, not suffocating!

Graduate Work: Some of what you need to know (and know how to do) will be known to you, while some will not. Identify sources of learning and get an annual plan on your calendar. For the second category (unknown unknowns) find some methods to explore other industries and organizations, and those that are either growing rapidly or rapidly declining, and see what might apply to your situation.

CHAPTER THREE

STRATEGY—THE WEAPON TO WIN THE BATTLE

n the last chapter we focused on the value of time and *The Five Levers of Success* that are imperative to leaving a lasting and positive imprint on your team and your business. In reality, we were laying the groundwork for you to have a stable platform to create a winning strategy. At the end of the day, it is the strategy that will be the largest difference maker and generate the biggest gap between you and your competitors.

The reality is that strategy wins wars, allows great leaders to run successful companies, and creates enormous wealth. The importance of a strategy cannot be overstated. But, actually creating and implementing a strategy is an entirely different animal. It is where the heavy lifting begins and it is where things can get a bit cloudy.

So with that said, here we go into the murky world of strategy. I hope that by the end of this chapter it will be less so. To get you started,

I have a quick story to share. A friend of mine had inherited a mess. His father had run a chain of grocery stores in another state and had passed away, leaving my friend to run the business. With ownership dispersed among quarreling family members who had different expectations, the only logical thing for him to do was to clean it up to the best of his ability, package the business, and then sell it and ride off into the sunset.

As he somewhat reluctantly jumped into his role as CEO and constant family counselor, he got some further bad news. Wal-Mart was coming to town with their grocery store concept. He did some research and discovered that on average, when Wal-Mart came to town, the juggernaut took a large chunk of business away from existing grocery stores. Since grocery stores run on very thin margins, a double-digit percentage loss of revenue would quickly send them into a pool of red ink!

With this rainstorm looming, my friend knew that his solution was not about working harder or executing better. It most certainly was not about "hoping for the best!" His vision didn't change, but the way he ran the business had to, or he'd be out of business in a flash. His response? Change his strategy. I'll show it to you later in the chapter.

For now, I'd like to answer four crucial and integral questions about strategy:

1. What is it?
2. Why is it important?
3. Why is it ignored?
4. How do I do it?

Strategic Snapshot: *When it comes to strategy, there is a myth that small companies cannot compete with global giants. But in my hometown of Boulder, Colorado a hardware store by the name of McGuckins holds their own, even with the large shadow of Home Depot just down the street. How* *many of you have a local hardware store near you that is flourishing? They keep the cash registers ringing because they have a unique way of competing. With more than 200,000 items in stock and a flock of "green vests" (their term for the knowledgeable employees on the floor—many of them former plumbers, electricians, etc.) they are hard to beat. One night many years ago, I had a critical light bulb burn out in an airplane that I was scheduled to fly. I had to replace it before my flight. I brought it into McGuckins. "I have one of those in back!" said the green vest. Somehow I knew that they would. Local hardware stores are not supposed to be able to compete anymore, but they prosper because they have a different strategy and execute it well.*

Companies like McGuckins recognize that they have a limited ability to compete with the name recognition and pure size of Home Depot. But what they do understand is their greatest asset may truly be their deep understanding of a smaller niche. They can provide more focused and attentive customer service with a knowledge-driven team that can likely solve problems that their larger and denser counterparts couldn't even touch.

The Language of Strategy

Vision is the prerequisite for strategy. I like to define vision as a "clear, compelling picture of the future that allows you to align the organization." Whether you are Google trying to "*…organize the world's information and make it universally accessible and useful*" or you are Southwest Airlines and attempting to "*…provide the best service and lowest fares to the short haul, frequent-flying, point-to-point, non-interlining traveler,*" you need to start by defining where you are going. It is your vision that acts as the destination point on your roadmap, while your strategy provides the path.

You might have a mission (defining what business you are in), stated values (defining how you will go about your business), a mantra, a purpose, a philosophy, a company song, and a mascot! That's all great, but if people can't answer the questions, "Where are we going?" (your vision) and "What are we going to do to get there?" (your strategy), then you are inevitably avoiding the hard work required to answer those questions.

Typically, a company founder has a vision. When he birthed the enterprise, there was a passion around his destination and the journey that he wanted to take. Some of you who are reading this book are in that camp. Your challenges are to find compelling language, make sure that it is achievable and representative of your goals, and then find people who want to take the journey with you. A vision is only as good as its clarity and the people that are projecting it. And that starts with you.

Most of you are likely not founders, but rather "professional" managers—hired guns that the shareholders have entrusted to create a financial return on their investment within their company. This does not mean that you have no responsibility in the company's vision. In fact, it is quite the opposite. That vision may have been passed onto you, but you still have the ultimate responsibly to be the beacon of that light.

What if there is no clear vision or your vision is no longer compelling? While you do not have to come up with one on your own by taking peyote and meditating in a sweat lodge, you are tasked with the responsibility of engaging your people in a conversation to develop that vision.

Ask them: "If you had a magic wand and could dictate the future of our business in a compelling way that provides tremendous value to our customers, what would you do?" A few weeks of dialogue around that question will bring forth some great ideas that you can work into a vision statement. However, don't avoid tough choices. A vision that encompasses more than one general direction is pointless.

The other option is to create the vision in your mind and then engage your team by getting their feedback and adjusting as you see fit. Some of you are more "visionary" than others. However, there has to be buy-in to the vision for it to drive behavior. You want commitment, not just compliance. Buy-in is best achieved by letting people have a voice, but repetitive messages, forceful and compelling communication, and rewarding behavior will also drive people toward your vision.

Visions are not everlasting, but they shouldn't change weekly! When yours is no longer compelling, sustaining, and in sync with the market, it is time to create a new one. If your vision and the actions that you are taking are not aligned, start the process of adjusting and rebalancing the equation.

Real Lesson: Whether you work on your own or in a collaborative fashion, start by answering the question, "Where are we going?" Leadership has obligations. As Edward Deming said, "management is about making predictions."

Execution is Not Strategy

"My strategy," the panelist said, "is to execute!" Unfortunately, a lot of heads in the audience nodded up and down. They were a group of CEOs—supposedly experts on strategy. I was the moderator and had not picked the panelist. I shook my head as well, but not up and down…

When asked how he would define pornography, United States Supreme Court Justice Potter Stewart said, "I know it when I see it." This, unfortunately, is the best definition that many executives have for strategy. When they see it, they can clearly tell you what it is. But leaders are not hired to point the finger and say "Aha!" Rather, leaders are hired to be the ones that build the strategy to create the response of "Aha!"

Even going back to ancient Greece, there are many definitions of strategy. If you put 100 CEOs in a room and ask them for a definition of strategy, you'll get 300 different answers. When asked what their strategy is, most CEOs cannot really define it.

Again, if vision is *where* you are going, strategy is *what* you will do to get you there. Vision is where, strategy is what. (Tactics are how, but we'll get to that later.)

There are two definitions of strategy that I like. One that consulting firm McKinsey lays claim to says that strategy is an aligned set of actions that allow a firm to successfully compete in its environment.

The other comes from the former CEO of Proctor and Gamble. He posits that to understand your strategy, you must answer two questions:

Where will we play?

How will we win?

You'll note that the two definitions above are action oriented and force you to make hard decisions. Strategic thinking requires decision making—saying yes to something and no to many others. It is *not* planning. You must plan to execute your strategy, but planning alone does not develop strategy.

It is also not execution, even though there's a saying that people pass around a lot: "It's all about the execution." This statement points to the notion that strategy doesn't really matter. But, of course, it does. Brilliant execution on the wrong strategy only makes you fail that much faster. As Sun Tzu said in *The Art of War*, "Tactics without strategy is the noise before defeat."

Strategic Snapshot: *Year after year, my publishing client continued to bang out great results in spite of all of the press about publishers going broke. However, he had a subsidiary that was in trouble. Growth was declining and their market segment did not appreciate the relevance of the books that they were selling. Better books were not going to save the day. Selling harder was not going to win the battle. They had to re-tool what they were doing and think of themselves as solving problems, not selling books. Within several years, they had multiple revenue streams offering multiple solutions to the problems of their marketplace. They had transformed themselves from a product company to a market-driven* *company with different strategy. And most important, they were back to double-digit growth!*

Strategy: My Father Never Had One

I sometimes work with second or third generation owners of private firms. "Why will people buy from you versus your competition?" I once inquired of a second generation CEO. He had recently gone through a "strategic planning" process, so the question seemed like a reasonable one. But he couldn't answer it.

His father actually had a strategy, but he didn't articulate it very well. As a result, everyone had to create his or her own answer to the question I had posed. More often than not, CEOs believe they have a strategy, but when asked to articulate it, it turns into a loose speech that doesn't really answer where they compete and why they'll win. They seem unfocused and if you ask them the same question ten times on ten different occasions, they'll likely give you ten different answers.

So why develop strategy? There are a number of reasons, but the most compelling one is that you must develop alignment *within* your team to make significant progress *for* your team.

I once worked with a highly paid management team in a large company that did not have a clear strategy. As industrious people abhor a vacuum, several of the senior people created their own assumptions around an assumed strategy. Two of these people who both had a large influence and very large budgets—the Chief Technology Officer and the Chief Marketing Officer—spent money like drunken sailors on competing projects and visions. The results were disastrous; they wasted large sums of money and literally accomplished nothing in the process.

Consider the graphic below. Imagine that A, B, and C are all small companies comprised of 7 people. Let's agree that all 21 people included are brilliant. Company A has 7 people all pulling in different directions. Company B has a pretty good degree of alignment around their strategy and makes significant financial progress. Company C has perfect alignment (which does not exist, but is a damn good objective) and makes great financial progress.

This diagram should give you a pretty clear representation of what can be achieved (or not achieved) if you have no strategy, a moderate strategy, and a hyper-focused one. We should all strive to create a well-considered and executed strategy, but even a little bit of momentum and thought in this area can pay big dividends.

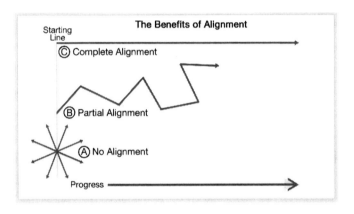

Strategic snapshot: *There is a group of do-it-yourselfers called the Maker Movement. These are not guys and gals who can just fix the sink. They are inventors, engineers and other creative souls who want to turn their ideas into cool stuff! You might address this market by selling them things. (In fact, the McGuckins' hardware store does!) But TechShop, a relatively new business, found a different way to monetize what this community wants. They are building community centers for these Makers that house everything from 3D printers to commercial sewing machines to plasma cutters and oscilloscopes. Their membership-based strategy brilliantly monetizes not only equipment and workspace needs, but also community! They are being rewarded for renting space, providing classes and access to*

specialized equipment, and for the relationships and sense of belonging that their members highly value.

Strategy: It Doesn't Require The Wisdom of Solomon

If strategy is so important, why do so many CEOs run from the topic? Many believe that they should be magically endowed with the Wisdom of Solomon when they accede to the big chair on mahogany row. It is frustrating and humbling to not have an answer to the most fundamental but difficult questions in business: Where are we going and what are we going to do to get there?

There are four fundamental problems with which leaders struggle when attempting to craft strategy:

1. ***It is messy.*** For each business environment, there are some bad strategies and some good ones, but there is no singular, right strategy, and the path to finding a good one is more like a meandering mountain trail than a drag strip. Most effective leaders want to take the most direct path to a solution—a great trait! However, crafting strategy requires you to explore multiple trails before you find the correct path to lead you to your destination.

2. ***It requires a process to develop.*** Carl Sandburg said, "Ordering a man to write a poem is like commanding a pregnant woman to give birth to a red-headed child." Likewise, I once worked for a CEO who took his top five people (I was one of them) and put us in a room to figure out our strategy. No facilitator, no process, just us guys. We had an 8-hour turf battle and produced nothing of value. There are many processes you can use to develop strategy and none of them are perfect, but you must use one. It is through the process that greatness is born.

3. *It requires a backbone.* Even in the face of the unknown, leaders have to make educated guesses. If you chose a path, you must say no to other paths. This is inherently difficult. You must be able to identify where you will spend your next dollar of investment, and choosing to spend a nickel in 20 spots is not usually a good idea. There are many vested interests inside a company. Without strong leadership, people will continue to do what they are currently doing rather than follow a new (and improved) direction. Once a strategy is chosen, you, the CEO, must be the lead advocate, salesperson, and—when required—traffic cop.

4. *It takes adjustments.* My wife is an artist who works in clay. She builds large pieces—often animals. While she has a picture in her head of what she wants it to look like when she starts, she makes adjustments as she produces the work. Sometimes pieces break before the clay is fired and they must be patched or reworked. Same thing with strategy. It is not always easy, but constant attention and adjustments will surely save the day.

Strategic snapshot: Exercise fads come and go faster than Jane Fonda can put on her leotard. However, in 2000, a guy by the name of Greg Glassman created something called Crossfit that took the fitness world by storm. Crossfit grew to over 10,000 gyms (they call them "boxes") in 12 years. The workouts themselves are worthy of an entire chapter, but what interests us is their strategy—"what" they are doing to grow the business, enhance health and well-being, and once again, monetize "community." The program, the boxes and Glassman's idea on how to make money are radically different from other "globo-gyms" and franchises. In fact, he passes up many opportunities for revenue simply to keep the system pure. Licensing the name, providing support and training to the box owners, all while allowing the individual owners complete flexibility is a long way from franchising.

Warning: If you engage in conversation with a Crossfitter, your eyes will glaze over before they quit talking about the benefits. Like the members of TechShop, Crossfitters are not just gym members; rather, they are members of a tight knit community (called a cult by some) who simply share a specific form of exercise as the platform.

Strategy: How Do I Do It?

You now know that you must have a vision, and a roadmap to execute your strategy. So how do you craft it? What do you do? There are many textbooks on strategy and it wouldn't hurt you to read a few. I have a bookcase full of strategy textbooks. But assuming you are a busy CEO, or soon-to-be CEO, and are looking for pragmatic advice, take a look at the chart below. Consulting guru Alan Weiss taught me this simple but effective technique for engaging people in a conversation around strategy.[1] It is only one of the techniques that I use with companies, but it is a good place for us to start.

---

1   Weiss, Alan: *Best Laid Plans—Turning Strategy Into Action Throughout Your Organization*, Las Brisas Research Press, 1994. *Organization.* Las Brisas Press, 1994.

On the vertical axis are what we'll call strategy components: product, service, relationship and distribution. Regardless of your business model, these are the areas in which you can compete.

Along the horizontal axis are the rankings or strategic importance of those components. One thing to note is that the competitive nature of your product or service will often decline over time. In nature, it is called entropy; in business, it is irrelevance. What is distinct and cutting edge today may be less-than-competitive and outdated tomorrow!

Why the lemons and tomatoes?

Well, remember my friend who inherited the grocery business? We are going to use his situation to explain how to use this simple tool. We'll do a post-mortem on his decision making process.

When he took over as CEO, lemons represented his business. His product was like everyone else's (canned beans are canned beans!); he offered no services, the relationships he had with his customers were undifferentiated, and his distribution model was like most grocery stores—brick and mortar locations on busy streets.

Then he heard that Wal-Mart was coming. He knew that he had to do something differently. He engaged his team in a conversation about how they could compete against a competitor that had a lower cost of doing business. How could they succeed while still charging more?

They realized that they could not effectively compete in the "middle of the store" where the cans of green beans resided. However, they could compete around the edge of the store where produce, meat and fresh foods resided, as Wal-Mart was not strong in those areas. They enhanced their produce and meat sections. They brought in local goods that Wal-Mart wouldn't carry. As their stores were in the Southwest, they brought in tortilla stands where fresh, hot tortillas were handmade on the spot.

They also wanted to differentiate how they interacted with their customers. They recognized that providing high levels of interaction was not Wal-Mart's strength, so they trained their coworkers to do some fantastic things.

The tomatoes represent their strategic profile after their strategic makeover, which allowed them to compete effectively with Wal-Mart and eventually sell the business for a nice price.

If you want to use this simple tool to look at your own business, here are the three steps:

1. *Evaluate.* Identify where you are on these dimensions. Don't delude yourself. If you think that you are distinct in a certain area, demand proof of yourself, or better yet ask your customers.
2. *Innovate.* Identify where you think that you can innovate to move from competitive to distinct or breakthrough. Problem solving can only keep you where you are; it will not help you move to the right. You must innovate. It is very unlikely that you can be distinct or breakthrough in more than one component, so you probably shouldn't try.
3. *Reinvigorate.* Your team will recognize the stormy clouds ahead. They are smart and perceptive and can read it on your face. So you have to lead. It is imperative to gather the troops to rally. An excited workforce will reinvigorate your business and support your innovations.

In this chapter, my goal was to pull the curtain back on the issue of strategy. This is not paint by numbers, nor is it like solving a math problem where if you apply the correct rules, you'll get the same answer every time. But think of this: each and every day your business is alive and breathing, your coworkers are coming to work and doing something. It is your job and responsibility to create a vision to ensure that they are doing something special. With a clear vision and strategy, you'll find yourself better positioned to succeed. Strategy is one of those words that is easy to talk about, but really hard to create and execute. So, if you can be crystal clear and project a compelling vision and craft a winning strategy, you have a launchpad for breaking free of the gravity of mediocrity. Then, of course, you need to execute! Guess what we'll cover in the next chapter?

Chapter Review:

Listen Up: Go talk to your troops and ask them questions like: "Where are we going?" and "Why do people buy from us instead of the competition?" Based upon the answers you obtain, you'll know whether or not you need to re-craft your strategy and clearly articulate your vision.

Quick Wins: Take the time to ask your senior team to identify the strategy of each of your major competitors, and then to assess the strength of your strategy vis-à-vis your competition. Using this type of measuring stick will help to ensure you are focusing on that which you can control.

Graduate Work: Ask a broad range of people to assess your current performance on the 12-box chart for each component. Identify where, based upon your core competencies, assets, and competitive situation, you think that you can gain a sustainable advantage on your competition. We'll talk about how to execute that idea in the next chapter!

 *READ TIME:* 12 min

CHAPTER FOUR

EXECUTION—THE DIFFERENCE BETWEEN DREAMS AND REALITY

I n the last chapter, we discussed the relationship between vision and strategy. We identified that you must know where you are going (vision) and *generally* what you will do to get there (strategy). But simply knowing what you will do to achieve your vision is often not enough.

I like to draw a hard line between strategy and execution (including planning) because crafting strategy is about *thinking* rather than planning and executing. However, if you cannot execute on those thoughts and those compelling ideas, then it is unlikely you will get anywhere! It's like saying, "I want to grow up and be a lawyer!" and then never attending law school, sitting for the bar, or even obtaining a job in the legal community.

So with that said, execution is about picking a good destination and then working to get there as quickly, efficiently, and accurately as possible.

In its simplest form, execution carries three specific yet crucial steps:

1. Clearly identifying objectives.
2. Taking action to meet those objectives.
3. Taking confirming or corrective action.

So with these in mind, let's shift our attention to exactly how these pillars interact with one another.

Step 1: *Clearly Identifying Objectives*

For our first crucial step in the overall concept of execution, we turn to the necessary practice of clearly identifying objectives. Have you ever finished a project and wondered whether you were really done or not? Or have you ever walked into an on-the-job performance review wondering how you were about to be evaluated? Have you ever been told to "jump" and wondered, how high is high enough? If so, you likely have been the victim of poorly articulated objectives. The direction in which we go should be based on our objectives, rather than just responding to random forces.

For example, many of you who read this book exercise daily at a gym or in your home. Most of you do this for a specific reason: You want to live longer, look better, or maybe even run a five-minute mile or bench-press 300 pounds. The clearer your objective, the higher your level of commitment. With apologies to Woody Allen, just showing up is not enough! Your objectives will drive your exercise program. Meandering around the gym doing random acts to create perspiration will not get you to a five-minute mile or a 300-pound bench-press. Only focused activity and persistence will do so, and it all starts with your objectives.

Objectives come in two flavors:

1. Musts; and
2. Wants

Let's consider another example. My wife and I love the outdoors and spend a lot of time in nature. However, after a few bear encounters, my wife is not so keen on sleeping in a tent. You can only imagine her feelings about sharing her sleeping quarters with that of a large furry animal. Outside of bear trouble, we also found that the act of backpacking was just getting to be more work than we wanted to do at any given time, so we decided to buy a small teardrop camper. The only two "musts" that we discussed were: 1) I could pull it behind one of our current vehicles and 2) We could sleep in it comfortably while staying warm and bear free.

So off we go to look at cute little campers with our simple objectives. Wouldn't you know it—we came home with something that had a toilet, air conditioner, refrigerator, kitchen, heater and shower. It even had an entertainment system, as it was standard "with the package." Talk about quite the up sale. After parking our new home on wheels in our driveway, I began to assess what had just occurred. I entered the dealership with two simple *musts* and exited with a fulfillment of a large amount of *wants*.

This behavior is far too common on, and off, the business field. It is literally an example of unclear expectations, and my wife's power of persuasion! We ended up making a purchase decision that encompassed our musts (that is a good thing!), but it also included many *wants*. The positive way to look at this is that we didn't miss on the expectations, we are just overachievers! When purchasing a vehicle, so long as you are not over budget, it is not a big deal. This is a luxury good and we viewed it as such. But if you applied this same behavior to business, who knows where you'd end up?

Too often, we end up making decisions that substitute our wants for our musts. That is like buying a new home that doesn't have the number of bedrooms that you need, but has a really cool swimming pool. Maybe the kids can sleep out there…

Real Lesson: We often fail in an endeavor because we did not take the time to adequately identify our objectives on the front end—both musts and wants. Slow the game down and take the time to really explore how you will define success.

So, let's get specific…

Remember our grocery store chain from the last chapter? Our CEO and his team had crafted a new strategy to effectively compete in their market by defining where they would play and how they would win—focusing on how they could differentiate themselves with specific products and customer relationships. But executing that strategy is something entirely different.

Let's take over for our overworked grocer. You're now the CEO. What does a win look like? You spend some time thinking about it, confer with your board of directors, and agree that there should be three objectives that this strategy achieves:

1. Revenue cannot decline by more than 5%. This is a tough one, as most businesses want to grow. However, with Wal-Mart coming to town, losing only 5% of revenue would be a big win based upon your research. You are going to find a way to increase efficiency and cut some costs so that you can achieve profitability at this sales level.

2. You want your EBITDA (earnings before interest, taxes, depreciation and amortization) to grow from 2% of revenue to 4% of revenue. Remember, you're in the grocery business, not selling iPhones! Once again, this would be a big win when

stacked up against your competition, and it is going to require higher gross margin, lower overhead, or both.

3. Because of your family situation, you would "like" to sell the business within three years. This will give you other opportunities and business endeavors on which you can focus, separating you from the difficult experience you've had with your family and in the business. It will also give your shareholders a successful exit vehicle and return on their investment.

Does this mean that these are the only three things that matter to you? Of course not! However, you are the CEO and must focus on the most important of changes and then align your plans and activities around your strategy to meet these objectives. Your strategy and your ability to execute that strategy must achieve these objectives.

In reality, these objectives were set before the strategy was even defined. If you are a hired gun (i.e. not the majority shareholder), it is very likely that you will be crafting strategy to meet objectives set by a board of directors or the owners of the company. The alternative is to execute the strategy and "see how far you can go."

Step 2: *Taking Action to Meet These Objectives*

Continuing with the example of the grocery store from the previous chapter, let's assume that you have a total of five grocery stores, each of which is divided into specific departments. You gather your store managers and their department managers (most likely the same team that you engaged to craft strategy) and decide exactly what you will do to execute your strategy. This is where planning comes into play and where the ideas become reality.

In proper sequence, here are the actions you would take all the way from creating a vision to executing your strategy:

1. **Vision**: You first have to create a vision. For our grocery stores, you and your management team worked to build upon your father's vision and did a bit of wordsmithing with the team, the end result being: "We will be the preferred choice for discerning grocery shoppers in our geographic area who want to be treated like a neighbor rather than a number."

2. **Strategy**: After the exercise detailed in the last chapter, you and your team decided on: "We will provide high quality, fresh products using local providers whenever we can. We will foster deep relationships with those customers who value the shopping experience and quality of product over cheap food."

3. **Critical issues**: You now must decide what significant changes are required for you to be successful. Critical issues are the two or three absolute "must do" changes that should take place in order for management to succeed in executing their strategy. In our case, you and your team concluded that the very most important things to do are:

   a. Build procurement capability to buy the very best fresh local products, especially in the produce and meat sections.

   b. Create a customer engagement framework that allows us to foster deep relationships with our customers.

   c. Design stores that stand apart from the traditional grocery experience and support the fresh and local concept.

This, by the way, is the defining line between strategy and execution. We are now going to move from "What" to "How," or from strategy to tactics. This shift is often where the greatest miss can occur. As we discussed earlier, strategy without execution is merely dreaming!

4. **Critical issue planning**: Great leaders must take each of those three critical issues and break them down into "bite size

chunks." In other words, who does what and by when. For example, some of the essential components of this are:

a. Milestones (major steps with due dates)
b. Resource requirements (e.g. people, capital, tools)
c. Specific tasks (i.e. major steps broken down into actions)
d. A project management tool (e.g. a method to track all of this—it could be an excel spreadsheet or an enterprise wide software program, heck it could be a notebook and pen if that will work for you!)

The key here is that these initiatives support management's strategy, and that they are incorporated into their operational planning and budgeting—that stuff that they would do even if they were not going to execute on a new strategy. Some critical issues may take several years to execute and some may be done in just months. For example, in the case mentioned above, the store design issue would most likely extend beyond the current year's budget and planning cycle.

5. **Operational planning and budgeting**: The next step to execution is considering the month-to-month, day-to-day planning and budgeting that management must do to run the actual business. Execution without boundaries can often lead to loss of profit. Make sure that critical issues are melded into these processes.

6. **Critical issue review process**: Critical issue plans should be reviewed in a formal way on a quarterly basis, and should occur separate and apart from whatever normal operational review processes management may already have in place. Remember that execution is fluid and you may need to adjust along the way.

7. **Operational review**: Most successful companies have monthly, quarterly and annual review processes in place to look at performance against their plans—both activities and financial. If there is a deviation from expectations, they quickly figure out why and do something about it!

8. **Strategy review**: When it comes to proper execution, the final step in the process is a periodic (e.g. annual) process to review strategy and answer the question: "Will our current strategy allow us to achieve our objectives and our vision?" However, strategy (unlike most planning exercises) doesn't fit neatly into one-year cycles. If leadership has reason to believe that the future as defined will inevitably change, they have a duty to re-evaluate where they are going and what they are going to do to get there. My best clients have built processes to constantly scan the horizon to look for changing customer expectations, new technologies, additional opportunities, and competitive threats. Some do this on an annual basis, and some as frequently as once per month.

In its truest sense, execution is taking action to meet objectives and goals. The eight specific actions mentioned above are where we turn dreams into reality, and position strong leaders to do the most for their respective teams and organizations. It is the constant reviews and adjustments that ensure the most seamless and clean transition and continuous development. Only when you truly have your ear to the stress and your finger on the pulse of your business can you effectively and efficiently execute at the highest of levels.

Step 3: *Taking Confirming or Corrective Action*
As mentioned earlier, as you continue to execute, it is crucial to pause often and assess the situation. It is imperative that you analyze

results to determine whether you are headed down the right path, or whether you need to take immediate and corrective action to right the ship. Great leaders are always adjusting to ensure that they are taking the correct actions so that the company reaches its desired outcome.

Imagine you buy a new dog—a very expensive golden Labrador that you purchased for companionship and to hunt pheasants. The dog comes from a wonderful lineage of labs; in fact, his mother and father were the Queen and King of the Westminster Kennel show. The puppy has been tested and has unusually high intelligence. You create a wonderful environment for him, give him all the toys he could want, and a nice place to play and sleep.

You have a long talk with your new dog and tell him your vision for the future and the skills that he will need to get there. You demonstrate how to roll over and even where to go to the bathroom—though the neighbors were not particularly happy about that!

However, for some reason, week after week, he continues to poop on your floor and has yet to even once retrieve the ball you throw for him. What could possibly be missing? He is smart, you gave him clear objectives, he comes from a good family, you work hard to train him, and yet he is not executing well.

Of course, you'd never get a dog to perform well without positive and negative reinforcement, yet we expect people and organizations to do it all of the time. You might hire smart people from great schools, spend time talking about what you need them to do, and provide them with all of the tools that they need, but they will still fail.

The truth is that if you want great execution, you need to reward the behavior that you desire and correct the behavior that you don't want. "Everyone knows that," you may say. Perhaps, but you would be amazed at the number of times that I've been asked to coach someone who is not performing at a high level, yet no one has given them that feedback! When it comes to your team, they can't fix what they don't know is broken. In fact, it is often worse than that; they have often been told that they were doing a great job when they weren't. That's like giving your dog a bone every time he poops on your Persian rug.

Real Lesson: If you want "X" results, reward people for X behaviors, not Y behaviors.

To recap, the three critical steps for execution are clearly identifying objectives, taking action to meet certain objectives, and taking confirming or corrective action. By following these three, you are paving the road to success.

Trust Good Process

Think of the processes in your business as the structure that supports everything else. Don't take them for granted! Take a look at the diagram below. This is an example of a process review that I used with a global company to do an assessment of their infrastructure. I use it to analyze the key processes in each crucial area so I can identify gaps and possible enhancements.

This very well run business had a remarkable track record of performance and wanted to continue that; however, they knew that the tools and processes that they used were in need of an upgrade. What works for a $100 million dollar company may not work for a $1 billion dollar company.

What key processes do you have in place to support each crucial area of your business? They need to be strong in order to support the weight and growth of the organization.

Real Lesson: Failure to execute (e.g. working to achieve your objectives) is most often a failure to create and adhere to an effective process.

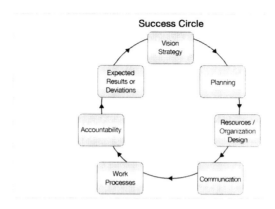

Whether in terms of a specific program, a small or large project, or simply when communicating with one another, when I work with CEOs and other executives who have failed to execute, I always look for gaps in setting objectives, the actions that they take, their process for reviewing progress, or what they do to either reward progress or take corrective action to right the ship. When things aren't going according to plan, it is easy to predict that one of these areas will be lacking.

The result of strong execution is even stronger results. It takes time to build the infrastructure and vital support necessary to continue implementing and developing simple (or not so simple) strategies. But time is limited. So when you focus your energy and direct your efforts in the right place, you begin to create a culture and environment that not only supports growth, but also nourishes it.

Real Lesson: Too many executives are fired for "failure to execute" and are dumbfounded as to what went wrong. If you start with good ideas (e.g. strategy or objectives) and follow the process I outlined here, you will have a much greater chance for success!

You are now equipped with the power to execute…in business. This chapter has laid bare the three crucial steps to effective execution. Start by clearly identifying your objectives so that you can begin to take specific and defined action to meet those objectives. Once you are working towards your goals, evaluate and decide where you need to take confirming or corrective action.

Chapter Review:

Listen Up: Take a critical look at your executive team (including you) and score yourselves on the three components of execution. You will undoubtedly uncover some things to work on.

Quick Wins: Start every project, initiative, or major action by clarifying your objectives—both musts and wants. Write them down. You'll be amazed and how much clarity this can bring!

Graduate Work: Take the success circle above and write down your key processes for each crucial area. On a scale of 1-10, how well are they meeting your needs? If you need to enhance some of them, take them one or two at a time and—if you'll excuse me—execute well!

CHAPTER FIVE

DON'T BRING A KNIFE TO A GUN FIGHT—THE LEADER'S TOOLKIT

Remember those classic episodes of MacGyver? You know, that superhero-esq scientist who would seem to combine the most uncommon items to save the day? The guy was a genius. He could disarm a bomb with a little bit of whiteout and a calculator. In every episode, he would pull off another miraculous feat in the most bizarre ways. From my perspective, leadership is the same way. We each have an amazing amount of talent, and must find ways to effectively deploy that talent within our organizations. But it is how we utilize the options and specifically how we combine them that can make the difference between good leadership and game-changing leadership.

To this point, you should have an understanding of the competencies that you must posses as a leader. Additionally, I've worked to give you a framework to use that allows you to analyze how you actually spend your time. Next, we discussed foundational understanding of strategy and how to think about where you will compete and how you will win. Lastly, you should have a good understanding of how to get things done and how to execute your strategy. That's a fantastic start for competence as a CEO! But there is more required when it comes to being an effective leader.

I have a son who served in the United States Marine Corp. My pride in his service is only matched by my gratitude for the training that he received. He saw combat and got into some messy situations, and while I appreciate his bravery and enthusiasm, his survival ultimately depended on him knowing how to use the tools of his trade. This chapter will cover the essentials that every leader needs to have in their toolkit—the tools that you must have available as CEO to assist you with the problems, opportunities, and decisions that you'll encounter. Bravery and enthusiasm are necessary to be an effective CEO, but to be truly successful you need to know how to utilize the tools your trade.

Leaders Start with a Solid Plan

Like firefighters, courageous leaders must often put out fires once they have started. However, lack of planning means that you'll always be fighting fires that could have easily been prevented. An old saying goes, "Lack of planning on your part should not mean a crisis on my part!" Don't let poor planning be the roadblock to success. Set an example for your employees by crafting and following solid business plans.

There are many books on planning, but if your organization is large, you don't have time to be a full-time project manager; you are a senior leader. You do, however, have to understand the planning process. If you are running a smaller organization, you may need to occasionally lead the planning process and personally manage a project. The process below should help you, regardless of which camp you are in. Once again, I am going to use a simple format.

Real Lesson: Consider the 7 elements below whenever you need to plan for a specific action or outcome, whether it is your work for the upcoming week, a specific project, or your spouse's birthday party.

The 7 Elements of Successful Planning

1. Define clear objectives (see previous chapter).
2. Identify the assets and skills required. If you don't have them, you need to develop or purchase them.
3. Assign ownership—that means that one person is ultimately responsible. Avoid dispersed ownership: When everyone is in charge, no one is!
4. Break down the project into smaller pieces so that it is more manageable. You will also be better able to track success.
5. Assign reasonable due dates for milestones.
6. Monitor progress—set up reasonable process and get it on your calendar.
7. Take corrective or affirming action depending upon progress.

You can use these elements as a template for any and every plan you develop, whether it is business or personal. Incorporating these seven elements into your planning process will help set you up for success.

The Distinction Between Planning and Responding

Running a business isn't easy; there will be challenges to overcome, which is why it helps to know how to effectively deal with those roadblocks. One big question is when to plan for vs. respond to the inevitable problems in your business. Here is a simple tool that might help you think about your daily workflow.[2] (If you're getting the message that simple often means effective, you are paying attention!)

---

2   A wonderful old book (originally written in 1965) that should be a "must read" for every CEO is *The Rational Manager* by Kepner and Tregoe.

	Cause	Effect
Responding	*Corrective Action*	*Adaptive Action*
Planning	*Preventive Action*	*Contingent Action*

As you can see, several of the actions that you have available to you are focused on events or problems that surfaced in the past—corrective action and adaptive action. They require reacting, not planning. Conversely, preventive action and contingent action require you to think about the future and plan for expected events. Consider the following example to better distinguish and understand these actions:

You run a consumer products company in a competitive space—the ski industry. Your strategy is to win by developing the most innovative products in your space—skiing equipment. In order to do this, you need the brightest, most creative people you can find on your product development team. Your competitors know this and your team members are ripe to being picked off. What do you do?

A corrective response is to wait until you lose someone and then scramble to find a replacement. An adaptive response is to spread the workload of your lost teammate onto the shoulders of her peers. These actions require little planning, but as is evident, they are not ideal solutions.

On the other hand, if you take preventive actions, you would have robust hiring practices, a healthy culture to reduce turnover, and a compensation package that is competitive. You might even locate your design team at the base of Aspen Mountain, and provide free season passes to your team—for daily product testing of course!

Contingent action is more like planning for the inevitable. In our example, you could find an outsource product development team. Additionally, you might try to keep your hiring funnel full of potential product developers by hosting fun events at the Outdoor Retailer trade show where you could woo your competitors' talented developers.

As you can see, there is a significant advantage to planning (preventive and contingent actions) vs. responding (corrective and adaptive actions). With that said, it is understood that you cannot plan for everything. This means that as a CEO you will need to be able to effectively plan *and* respond.

Real Lesson: Many companies rely on adaptive behavior for challenges that should have been either prevented or corrected. An easy way to find examples of this is to talk to your newly hired employees and ask them, "What do we do around here that seems a bit crazy?" Their answers will reveal the "workarounds" that you don't even see anymore. Some are harmless and some are costing you lots of money!

For the most effective plan, it is imperative that you tie three things together:

1. Your strategy
2. Your "to do list" (in whatever format you keep it)
3. Your calendar

This will ensure that you are working on the right stuff (i.e. driven by strategy not by the most recent text message), that you have taken the time to break it down into bite size chunks (your to do list), and that it gets onto your calendar so that it will get done!

You should always be working from a plan, while understanding that nothing goes exactly as planned.

Real Lesson: Remember to spend some time each week planning your work. Don't let inbound phone calls, emails, and text messages—or for goodness sake, social media—control your activities.

Decision Making

There is no room in the C-suite for executives who are afraid of making decisions. I'd rather make 100 decisions and only get 90 right than make 50 "perfect" decisions. Perfection is truly the enemy of success!

"I have a problem that I'd like to discuss" is something that I hear frequently from clients. In reality, what they really have is a difficult decision. As I learned from *The Rational Manager,* most problems follow a similar formula: They are a deviation from expectations for which you don't know the cause, and they matter. (If you don't really care, it's not much of a problem.) This explanation should help you clarify the difference between a problem and a decision, which is important because the solution is different for each.

For example, you might have a "problem" with one of your Vice Presidents. She doesn't play well with others, she misses deadlines, and she doesn't take direction well, but she produces good results. Quite a problem, right? Wrong! What you have is a decision to make. You need to explore your options (e.g. fire her, rehabilitate her, put up with her) and make a decision. Here is how:

What follows is a simple format that will serve you very well when making important decisions. You'll see some common language from previous sections. (I love it when it all starts to come together!) I suggest you memorize this—it may help to use the acronym **OAR** to remember it. For this example, we will use our "problem" executive.

1. **Objectives**
   a. Musts:
      i. Stop irritating the other senior executives
      ii. Meet deadlines

      b. Wants:
         i. To keep her on the team
         ii. For her to take direction graciously from you
2. **Alternatives**
      a. Rehabilitate her
      b. Fire her
3. **Risks** (including expense or investment required)
      a. Alternative "a"
         i. Your time
         ii. Low chance for success
         iii. Continued disruption on the senior team
      b. Alternative "b"
         i. Potential short term loss of revenue
         ii. Disrupting her team
         iii. The expense of recruiting a new Vice President

The **OAR** format allows you to simply and effectively break down your decision options. Whether you are considering a merger, a new product, a new banking relationship, or terminating a Vice President, the **OAR (objectives, alternatives, risks)** model will serve you well.

Problem Solving

You probably have, in part, been promoted because of your ability to remain calm under pressure and to solve problems. As CEO you'll now get the stickiest, messiest, and most pervasive problems, so you need to be knowledgeable about problem solving.

Remember, a problem is a something that does not meet expectations, and you don't know why. It also is big enough to go beyond being a nuisance, meaning it becomes something material enough to care about.

What exactly is problem solving? It is returning to a previous state after taking corrective action. Problem solving looks like this:

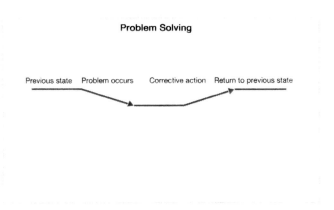

As you can see, problem solving, by definition, is the work required to:

a)   Notice a deviation
b)   Identify the problem
c)   Take corrective action

The objective in problem solving is to get back to the previous state. (If your desire is to improve on the previous state, you'll need to go beyond problem solving and innovate.) Problems are all the result of a change, with one exception—a "newborn" problem. An example would be a new product that does not sell as well as expected. In that case you have no base-line performance level and it is possible that your expectations or assumptions are the problem.

Much like decision-making, it is critical that you have a working framework to solve problems. Below is a simple and effective framework that I adapted from *The Rational Manager.*

	Is	Is Not	Distinctions	Changes
What	The southwest region of your multi-unit grocery store business has shown dramatic reduction in growth	The other six regions are not seeing this decline in growth	~The problem is confined to a specific area ~Isolated leadership ~Unique competitive environment	~Recent culture survey shows less engagement in this region ~New competitor is executing aggressive expansion plan ~Reduced marketing budget last year in this region ~New Vice President in charge of region Q3 of 2013
Where	Decline is specific to this region	Good growth in other states and regions	Isolated geography	
When	Started Q1, 2014	Prior to that point, consistent growth	Sales growth was robust prior to this period, now consistently poor	
Extent	80% of stores in this region are showing decline	2 districts within this region are still doing well	2 "successful" districts have different marketing plans	

Steps:

1. **Decide** whether this is a problem or a decision. (In the above case, the declining sales growth is a problem as it is a deviation from expectations, you don't yet know the cause, and you care.)

2. **Clearly define** what the problem is and is not, as well as where and when it occurs and the extent to which it occurs.

    a. Do NOT try to solve at this point. It is critical that the problem be clearly defined first. (In this case, the problem might be the VP's weak leadership, changing consumer trends, changes to marketing, or it might be competition.)

3. **Identify** distinctions. Do not cluster multiple problems together.

4. **Identify** changes that have occurred. All problems are a result of a change, unless it is a "newborn" problem (e.g. a new product that does not sell well).

5. **Create** possible assumptions as to the cause.

6. **Test** the most likely assumptions until you find one that matches the clearly defined problem (both IS and IS NOT).

7. **Look** for either Corrective or Adaptive actions.

You'll have to work through this a few times before it becomes natural, but eventually this 7-step problem solving formula will be one of the best tools in your toolkit.

While we are talking about problems, let's focus on how to avoid creating a monster. Since you are the top dog and have executive power, everyone will want you to solve their problems. Trying to solve every problem is a big mistake! What you want, within reason, is for people to solve all of their own problems (within their limit of authority).

The magic formula for making this happen is to respond as follows when someone brings you a problem:

"Please describe the problem for me."

"Tell me what options are available to solve the problem."

"Which option do you think is best and why?"

Responding in this manner will push your employees to think issues through more thoroughly before they ask for help, and ultimately it will teach them how to solve their own problems.

Culture: A Tool, Not a Result

"Son, if you really want something in this life, you have to work for it. Now quiet! They're about to announce the lottery numbers."
—Homer Simpson

Creating a healthy culture is not like winning the lottery; you have to work for it. But what is "it?" How do we define culture?

I've heard many of definitions of "culture," and most of them are not satisfying. We need to go beyond traditional definitions and think of culture as a tool to achieve results, instead of looking at it *as* a result. Building organizational culture is not passive; it takes action. For our purposes, you can define culture as the sum of the behaviors that you reward or allow.

Sorry for this reference ladies, but I've been in too many guys' restrooms where there is a framed document over the urinal—usually with an eagle or the Constitution embossed on it—stating the following:

"We are truthful, hard working, industrious, compassionate, good looking and truthful business people who adore our boss and live to make him rich."

Admittedly that is a slight exaggeration, but it is not too far from the truth. However, culture is not words on a page: It is the sum of the actions that are rewarded and allowed in your company, regardless of the speeches you give, the shareholders' letter in your annual report, or the framed documents hanging over your urinals in the office.

If you pay for high performance and make heroes out of those who go the extra mile, you will have a high performing culture. If you *say* you expect high performance, but allow your buddy Vince to hang on to his job even though he is a slug, your culture is one of "suck up to the CEO and you won't get fired."

If you want to figure out what your culture is, you might start by asking your employees two questions: "What do you get fired for around here?" and "Who are the heroes in our company?" If you don't have a culture of honesty (which rewards or allows people to speak the truth to the people in power), then you'll need to get someone like me, who has made a consulting career out of speaking the truth to those in power, to ask those questions and get the real answers.

If you find out that your existing culture isn't exactly high performing, there are steps you can take to improve your company culture.

Real Lesson: Do you want to change your culture? Here is the four-step formula:

1. Define the culture you want.
2. Attract the right people.
3. Build commitment through vision, strategy and personal behavior.
4. Cement the behavior you want through management practices: rewards and punishments.

As you think about the culture that you want to have, you might think in terms of dichotomies to help you make important and effective changes. Here is a list to start from:

Kind	Nice
Family	Team
Transparent	Need to know
Risk takers	Risk averse
Meetings	Memos
Fun	Serious
Performance	Relationships
Competitive	Supportive
Work long hours	Balance
Take credit	Humble
Value long term results	Value short term results
High tolerance for ambiguity	Low tolerance for ambiguity
High tolerance for stress	Low tolerance for stress
High tolerance for conflict	Low tolerance for conflict
Mission matters	Metrics matter
Competitive	Collaborative
Process driven	Innovation driven
Speed	Correctness

There are three "types" of dysfunctional cultures that I encounter most frequently:

1. **Nice vs. Kind.** This was covered in Chapter One regarding leadership, so I won't redefine it here, but suffice it to say that what can plague a leader can plague an entire organization. When speaking the truth is quietly outlawed so that people are not upset, it results in missed opportunities, ineffective behavior that goes unchecked, and poor financial results.

2. **Compliant rather than committed.** This is a direct result of the CEO's actions. Commitment is driven by people understanding what is important (e.g. clarity of vision and strategy), by

employees being able to do their job with support (not micro-management), and by recognition. Compliant organizations are driven by controlling leaders who create a culture of little fun and mediocre results.

3. **Metrics over mission.** A friend used this phrase right before he left the company he was working for. I asked him what had changed, as he had been a committed executive for some time. He replied that metrics had become much more valued than the mission of the company.

Take these examples of dysfunctional culture into consideration when evaluating your own company culture. Remember that high performing cultures are those that reward hard work, commitment, and truth.

Real Lesson: Consider these top 10 principles for a highly effective culture:

1. Culture starts at the top, so look in the mirror.
2. You must define culture with clear language.
3. Culture is what you reward and allow. Don't just let it happen.
4. Systematize it: Hiring, communication, rewards, and punishment.
5. Hire slow and fire fast.
6. Don't be a copycat: Your culture can be unique.
7. The first sale is to yourself. Convince yourself of the ROI.
8. Don't espouse X and do (or allow) Y.
9. Look under the hood—measure and codify your culture.
10. Dramatic action is needed for dramatic change.

Your toolkit now includes the essentials for building a high performing culture that will yield high results.

The Sharpest Tool In The Shed—The Question

There is not one best way to lead, but there are many ways that are more effective than others. As psychologist Daniel Goleman[3] pointed out, some styles of leadership—coercive and pacesetting—are actually net losers. Instead, you want to use the four other styles that he identifies—authoritative, affiliative, democratic and coaching— to bring positive results to your organization.

There is a time to tell and a time to query. As an effective leader, you must be able to strongly state your convictions regarding vision, strategy, and values. In addition, you must also be capable of asking brilliant questions to engage the minds of others. Remember, you want commitment, not just compliance.

As Stephen Covey said, "Seek first to understand, then be understood." I've worked with many leaders throughout my career and I've noticed that those who are most effective at generating great ideas, enthusiasm and commitment are those who are most committed to asking great questions. Henry Ford corroborates this saying, "If there is any one secret of success, it lies in the ability to get the other person's point of view and see things from that person's angle as well as from your own." Learn how to see things from others' perspectives and start asking great questions.

Real Lesson: Leading by making liberal use of questions is more effective than spouting pronouncements. Questions build commitment, foster learning, and reduce defensiveness.

As I transitioned years ago from being a business leader to working as a consultant and coaching CEOs, I had to learn how to ask questions. The fact that I had lots of experience running things, and often had what I believed to be a great answer to a conundrum that a CEO was facing, didn't prove effective. Yes, occasionally I can provide advice that

---

3   Goleman, Daniel. "Leadership that gets results." Harvard Business Review, March—April 2000.

is accepted and actionable, but most often the best way to help others is to ask questions and let them discover the best path forward—with a little nudging along the way. The same holds true for you as CEO.

Here is a short list of some of the best questions that you can use on a frequent basis.

1. Given our strategy, what are the top three challenges that we are facing?
2. What is the most important thing that you can do this week to add value to the company?
3. What can I do to help you succeed?
4. If you were in my position, what would you do?
5. Why? (Perhaps the best question of all time!)
6. What do you like best about your job?
7. What are we doing around here that is a waste of time?
8. If you had to do that in half the time, what would you do?
9. If you had twice as much budget, how would you spend it?
10. If you had a magic wand, what would you do to address this problem?
11. If you had no constraints, what would you do?
12. What is the one thing that you can do right now to help this situation?
13. If you owned the company, what would you change?
14. Who do you think is the most valuable person on our team and why?
15. What do you think that I need to hear that everyone is afraid to say?

Remember that as a leader, the quality of the answers you get will always be directly correlative to the thoughtfulness of the questions you ask. So, ask a better question to get a better answer. Always look at yourself as a modern day MacGyver, with an endless amount of resources and tools at your disposal. Good leaders know they have the actual tools, great leaders know how to use them.

Chapter Review:

<u>Listen Up</u>: You need to think about having a consistent set of tools that you can use as a CEO. The five included in this chapter are *Planning, Decision Making, Problem Solving, Creating Culture, and Asking Questions.* Master these and then look at what else you need to be successful. Mastery comes from use, not from just reading about them!

<u>Quick Wins</u>: I have at my ready some "cheat sheets" of common processes that I use frequently. They have saved my bacon more than once. For instance, the OAR technique for decision-making can be very valuable. You also might think about creating a list of questions that you can carry with you.

<u>Graduate Work</u>: There is no better way to understand something than to teach it. Once you are confident in your ability to use these tools, teach them to your team!

CHAPTER SIX

PLAYING CHESS ON THE BULLET TRAIN—THE MARRIAGE OF VELOCITY AND LONG TERM THINKING

With your toolkit in hand, we now shift to understanding the relationship between velocity and long-term thinking. As a leader, things move fast. In fact, they move faster than fast, often gaining velocity, and sometimes feeling like a runaway train. As an added bonus, we are then required to begin an exhilarating game of chess while that train is travelling in full motion and at full speed. But that is just half the fun of leadership. Great leaders are those who not only weather the circumstances, but who are also smart enough to optimize them.

We live in a global economy that is supported by technology. Continuous advancements have made communication instantaneous and also addicting. There is constant pressure to stay informed and up-to-date, especially in the business world. Things move fast, and technology makes them move even faster. I was talking recently with a company executive for whom I was facilitating a strategy session and we both chuckled when, at a break in the action, all 10 participants immediately pulled out digital devices to check emails, voice messages, text messages and perhaps even Facebook.

It used to be that when a break was taken, everyone rushed out to pay phones in the lobby or grabbed a copy of the newspaper to find out what was going on in the world. That may sound quite bizarre if you are under 55, but it is true! In today's digital age, staying current has taken on a new meaning.

The speed of business and simply the speed of life are growing exponentially. Life is fast and as a result, velocity in business has sped up, and will only continue to increase. The trick to navigating and trailblazing in this environment is threefold:

1. Increase the velocity of your business.
2. Stay plugged in to the right information surrounding you.
3. Slow the game down to explore the right things.

Velocity Explained

Velocity is an interesting word. In economics it is the turnover of money—how fast a buck, euro, rupee or bitcoin makes its way through the economy in a given amount of time. In physics, velocity is speed with a directional component. Both of these definitions have significance to a wise business leader.

From the physics' definition, we might assert that you can only develop velocity by moving in the right direction. Spinning around in circles is lost energy. If your movement is random, you might occasionally hit upon a good direction and it will look like progress, but it is short lived and dependent upon luck. The direction you choose equates to your vision and your strategy. The speed is how well you execute. (In other words, the previous chapters on strategy and execution are critical!)

Strategy=direction
Execution=speed (and accuracy)

In economic terms, our country's output (gross domestic product) is a function of the money supply multiplied by velocity. In business, our output is a function of our assets multiplied by financial return. Within reason, the faster you can generate a return on your assets—in our case hard assets such as property, plant, and equipment, as well as soft assets such as intellectual property and people—the better off you are. Likewise, the fewer assets that you use to generate profit, the better your return. When you get a faster or greater return than your competition, it provides cash for you to reinvest in other products and projects, thereby giving you a competitive advantage or a healthier rate of return for your shareholders.

Leveraging speed is about changing your perspective. As an example, I have a friend who's the CEO of a large organization, and he wanted some software written to solve a problem. His internal team of 300 told him it would take a year. He got it done in a week by posting a requirements document on the web and taking bids. Sometimes it pays to utilize outside resources.

High Velocity in Organizational Performance

Think about increasing the velocity in your business by reducing roadblocks that can often get in the way of your momentum. There are three major impediments to high velocity in organizational performance.

1. **Direction**—The first is about direction. We often confuse process with objectives. They're significantly different. For

instance, I sometimes get calls from people who want me to facilitate an "off-site strategic planning meeting." When I ask why, I often find that the real objective is: a) to fill time, b) to continue with the tradition, c) to entertain the troops, or d) unknown. Not one of those is a good reason. When I pursued a line of questioning recently with an executive who initially wanted a "strategic planning session," the need I uncovered had to do with a companywide lack of accountability, which required a different solution.

If you first clearly identify the objective by asking hard questions, you can then determine how to address the issue most effectively. Ask "what" first, then "how." I don't care how fast you are, if you work on the wrong thing, you won't see the results you want.

2. **Time**—Second, you can often achieve the objective much more quickly than your initial assumption (like my friend with the software issue). It's helpful to ask, "What if we had to do this in 10% of the time we allocated?" Once you survive the initial incredulous looks, you might come up with some very unique answers and save a lot of time.

3. **Success**—In the end, it's about success, not perfection. Oftentimes, squeezing out the last 10% of a project can take an inordinate amount of resources and time with little or no increase in quality. Clearly define the objective and meet it.

In addition to being a critical lever, velocity also has a dark side. Think back to the economy for a second—in this case, velocity is good, but if the velocity of money is very fast, we have inflation. A little inflation is a very good thing, where as a lot of inflation is a bad thing— it basically creates chaos.

In a company, a consistent, healthy long-term return is a beautiful thing. Whereas shooting for short-term results can cause chaos and damage your ability to succeed over the long-term.

Real Lesson: Velocity (speed and proper direction) in business can be a huge competitive advantage! However, you must keep your eye on the long-term success of the organization. Be conscious of tradeoffs!

Leadership Boom

A common definition (and one that I like) says that management is about taming complexity and leadership is about driving change. If so, then it is clear that to move forward and adapt to the rapid rate of change we are all experiencing, we need more leadership. This is one of the paradoxes of business— you must both produce management structure and systems to be able to run your business on a day-to-day basis, and also have the leadership skills to be able predict changes and nimbly respond. In other words, you need to continually build structure while at the same time consider tearing it down and doing it differently. (Get used to the ambiguity; it's why you get paid the big bucks!)

Too often leaders play it "safe." Rather than guess wrong about the changes needed to prosper in the long term, they move more slowly than the changing business situation requires, and then blame their competitive environment. In the end, playing it safe is not safe. If you need proof, just look at Kodak, the music industry, or the newspaper industry.

Real Lesson: You must move at, or above, the rate of change (the sum of customer needs, competition, changes in technology and regulation) outside the company to continue to win. You're not playing solitaire—you're playing chess!

Years ago when I transitioned from flying single engine airplanes to complex, multi-engine aircraft, I remember the awful feeling of being "behind the aircraft" on my early flights. Things happened much faster and there were a lot more instruments on the panel. There were more levers as well and if you pulled the wrong one at the wrong time, you were likely to go "clunk" and ruin your whole day. And just like with your business, there was no way to pull over to the curb—you had to think way ahead of the aircraft.

Riding the Bullet Train

In today's age, you're basically trying to play a strategic game of chess while riding a bullet train at high velocity, which is not an easy feat. So, what is the best way to handle this situation?

Based upon our earlier definitions of problem solving and decision-making, what we have here is not a problem, because we know the cause. Instead, we have a decision to make, which means we need to utilize our OAR model (Objectives, Alternatives, Risks).

We have two objectives:

1. We *must* avoid going "clunk" in the medium or long term.
2. We *want* to maintain current growth and profit. This is a "want," as it is possible that we do some investment spending now that will pay off later.

We have a number of possible permutations, so to help break them down, we will put them into sections that are understandable. The following chart includes some alternatives with the associated risks. Remember, risk also includes cost.

Alternative	Risk (plus cost)
Chug along: Continue to operate as if nothing is going to change.	While not frequently verbalized in this fashion, this is a typical default position. It has the advantage of no new costs, and feels "safe;" however, while this may work for some period of time, you may be heading towards irrelevancy. There is risk of a disruptive technology, new competition, or a change to your business model that could have been predicted and acted upon. Some industries (not many) see very little change and if you are in one, this may be safe… for a while.
Fast follower: Wait for a significant change to happen and then make a dramatic shift.	This also allows you to avoid any new costs, but carries the significant risks of a) not being able to change fast enough when the platform shifts, and b) being a "me-too" player without the ability to identify how you win or where you play.
Go shopping: Assume that you can "buy" (e.g. merger or acquisition) whatever new technology or competency is required to compete in the future.	No current cost here, but you'll need a healthy balance sheet to do this, so watch those shareholder distributions! You may also find that whatever you try to buy is not available. Finally, while some companies do it well, merger or acquisition activity usually destroys company value.

Find a guru: Hire a consulting firm to tell you what the future looks like—specifically, what your strategy should be and how to execute.	Too bad it is not that easy, though many make this mistake. This is like buying a book on boxing and assuming you'll win the fight. This option carries high risk, is very expensive, and is not scalable (i.e. they'll be back next year for another assignment).
Own it: Build internal capability to scan the horizon for changes and expose yourself (and your team) to as many sources of information as is reasonable, including adjacent industries and others with similar characteristics.	This has some cost associated with it. It also requires a good deal of discipline because it is not current revenue generating activity. It also forces you to "think strategically" on a frequent basis and consider actions that are counter to your current operations.

You may have some other options, but I hope that you see my point. If you ignore your velocity and the potential for change, you are introducing tremendous risk into your business.

Real Lesson: It is malpractice for a CEO not to think about the future.

If you are going to maintain, or increase, the velocity at which you are traveling, there are a few things that I suggest you consider:

1. *Get out of your office and explore the competitive environment around you.* Also look at adjacent industries. Grab a few meetings every month with other leaders and ask them what they are seeing. Most importantly, however, you should do whatever you can to see your business from the viewpoint of the customer.

2. *Put mechanisms in place for your team to scan the horizon for trends, new technologies, regulations, etc.* You need a constant assessment of the environment and your ability to compete. Leadership and change authority John Kotter suggests that we need two systems in our organizations, one to operate our day to day business and one to scan the future and respond—a constant evaluation of our strategy.[4] Below is a base list that will help get you started. Feel free to add to it or subtract from it as needed.

   - Customer needs and buying patterns
   - Political trends
   - Economic trends
   - Social trends
   - Technology trends
   - Workplace/employment practices
   - Top competition profile
   - Manufacturing process
   - Product design (process and features)
   - Sales/Marketing methods
   - Distribution methods
   - Anticipated financial environment
   - Critical inputs availability (e.g. natural resources, components)

3. Ask yourself and your team, "If we had to do this twice as fast, how would we do it?" In this case, we define "it" as specific functions (e.g. hiring, product development), or the critical elements of the business model (e.g. getting to market with new products, serving customers, etc.).

---

4 Kotter, J. "Accelerate!". *Harvard Business Review.* November 2012.

4. Figure out what you can speed up and what you need to slow down. Yes, some things should probably be slower. For instance, you need to find time to think about the future rather than just experiencing today.

5. You need to be skilled at synthesizing data and looking for trends. Information is not the same as knowledge, and you need to turn data into knowledge that is actionable.

6. You must take a sharp knife to the time suckers that exist, whether on your calendar or not. My experience is that almost every executive can find an additional four-eight hours in his or her workweek by eliminating non-value-add activities.

7. Get rid of, or outsource, the non-value-add activities throughout your organization. This may include entire departments. You cannot cut your way to greatness, but you also cannot afford to have a lot of friction on the tracks slowing down the train.

8. Stay current on technology for both personal effectiveness and shifts in your industry. Get your Vice President of Technology to spend an hour a week tutoring you to make sure that you are current.

9. Ask yourself and your team, "If speed were our only competitive lever, what would we do differently?"

You purchased this book to become a better leader. But as a leader, you have a continuous responsibility to work towards constant self-evaluation, always determining if you are willing and able to move at, or above, the pace of business around you. If you determine things are moving a little too fast around you, I believe that you have a moral obligation to your customers and your company to let someone else run the company. It is with unparalleled passion and drive that you should continue your path towards becoming a seasoned and high-impact leader.

Chapter Review:

<u>Listen Up</u>: Look at the top three critical processes in your business (i.e. those that are most important to executing your strategy) and figure out how to do them faster.

<u>Quick Wins</u>: Put together a committee of smart people with open minds who spend part of their week looking at current trends, future threats, and opportunities. Then have them interact with your senior executive team at a breakfast meeting once per month.

<u>Graduate Work</u>: F. Scott Fitzgerald said that intelligence was the ability to hold two competing thoughts in your head at the same time and still function. Think about how you can slow the game down (i.e. focus on the critical), and at the same time use velocity as a competitive advantage.

CHAPTER SEVEN

THE CHICKEN CAME FIRST— YOU NEED A HEALTHY ORGANIZATION TO PRODUCE PROFITS

A s this is a book about leading a business or an organization, it cannot be complete without talking about profit. For our purposes, the terms "business" and "organization" refer to the enterprises that I'm helping you lead more effectively. Most everything in this book applies to both businesses and other types of organizations, but we must take a slight departure here because for capitalism to work, businesses must make a profit.

Other types of organizations may exist without profit because they receive funds through benevolence or distributions facilitated by the government. However, a for-profit business requires that those in charge figure out how to provide value to the marketplace that exceeds the cost of its inputs.

I admire many leaders and organizations that are of the not-for-profit variety, but I am also an avowed capitalist. Capitalism has driven more benefit to humankind than all do-gooder organizations combined. While there are many people who believe capitalism is bad, I believe that their viewpoint is naïve. A company only benefits society when it produces a profit. With that said, my guess is that if you bought this book, I am preaching to the choir; therefore, I'll leave it to others to more skillfully address the benefits and ethics of capitalism.

As a business leader, you will no doubt be held accountable, and probably rewarded, for producing healthy financial results. Unfortunately, some of you are probably being rewarded to *maximize* profit over the short term rather than *optimize* profit over the long term. There are far too many books out there on getting rich quick. I'd like for you and your shareholders to get rich, but in a sustainable fashion.

The money I've made over the past 40 years has been based in great measure upon the financial results I have achieved as a business owner, senior executive, board member and independent advisor to other executives. Sometimes I stumbled, but over all I did well. I'd like to share some of the most important lessons that I've learned from those experiences. No GAAP or FASB spoken here, just five financial leadership lessons applicable to top leaders.

Financial Lesson # 1: *Profit is the egg, not the chicken!*
It takes a healthy business to produce a profit over the long haul. The business is the chicken; the profit is the egg. As such, you need to focus on the health of the chicken to produce good eggs.

When you want to water your garden and nothing comes out of the end of the spout, you probably immediately realize that there is a kink somewhere in the hose. When water comes out but not at the rate expected, you might determine you have a leak or two in the hose. Demanding more water to come out without fixing the hose won't do a single thing. Yet, many business executives and owners are screaming for more water when they should be fixing the hose.

I was fortunate to work in an environment for 20 years where we understood that if we focused on customer satisfaction, the engagement of our coworkers, the health of the organization, AND rewarded people for financial results, good things would happen. We focused on the chicken and out popped healthy eggs!

Real Lesson: Profit is the result of an effective strategy, a healthy organization and great execution. It is not the result of spending all of your time thinking about profit. If you weigh yourself every day without changing your exercise or diet, you will not lose weight.

Financial Lesson # 2: *Buy a pair of hands, get a brain for free!*

I have been a fan of Apple products for decades, and I love the Steve Jobs story as much as anyone else. However, as someone who coaches CEOs, one of the things that concerned me about Jobs was that others would try to emulate his style; let's call it "One Big Brain In A Black Turtleneck." OBBIABT might have worked for Jobs, but *he* really was the smartest guy in the room—perhaps in all of Silicon Valley. If you believe you are just as smart as him and merely want to emulate his style, then I'm not sure why you bought this book. However, my guess is that you do admire him and his success, but are hoping to achieve your own goals with the help of some expert advice.

So, how do you produce great financial results when you don't have all of the answers? You have to engage the minds of your people. As an old boss of mine used to say, "When you hire a pair of hands, you get a brain for free!"

Many years ago, Jack Stack wrote a great book on open book management called, *The Great Game of Business.*[5] The synopsis of the book is:

- Company in trouble with a new leader
- Leader can't figure it out on his own
- Realizes that the people on the shop floor are knowledgeable but not engaged
- Shares all financial and operating data with them and asks them how to fix the company
- Boy gets girl, gets married, and lives happily ever after

Only the last bullet point is a fib; but you get the picture. If you involve your people in running the business and show enough trust in them to share the numbers, you'll go much further than when trying to use the OBBIABT methodology.

Implementing open book management takes some work, so if you are going to do something transformational in this regard, my suggestion is that you use the following steps:

1. Cleary identify the problem or opportunity. You can rally people around either end of the spectrum—right the sinking ship or achieve a brighter future.

2. Tell them that they are going to help you achieve some goals. You will share all of the data with them, which means your futures are tied together. This also means you will share the rewards with them.

3. Create a method (e.g. a training program) to develop financial literacy (i.e. to make sure that everyone knows how to read an income statement).

---

5   Stack, Jack. (1992) *The Great Game of Business.* New York, New York: Doubleday

4. Bring them together to share the information on a frequent (e.g. monthly) basis and facilitate problem solving or innovation to achieve your objectives.

5. Reward them based upon results.

Like everything else, this sounds simple, but it isn't easy. I have implemented this type of program and seen some of my clients adopt this methodology with great results, but it requires a bit of faith, some good process, a willingness to share the rewards, and a lot of trust. If you don't have those four characteristics, either develop them first or—as they say on TV—don't try this at home!

Real Lesson: Regardless of whether or not you adopt open book management, you need to engage your people and make use of their energy and ideas. Town hall meetings, one-on-ones, walking the shop floor, and a "great ideas contest" are all viable tools; but what is most important is that you really want to hear from them, that you want them to participate in the success of the company, and that you listen and act. If you do this only as a window dressing, you'll lose credibility and get worse results. So, if you are going to try open book management, you have to truly believe it will work.

Financial Lesson # 3: *Grow Wisely*

There is a saying often used in the business world that if a shark stops swimming, it will drown. Well, it is only true for certain types of sharks, but it is still a darn good analogy! If a business tries to tread water, bad things happen.

Several times in my career I have seen owners of businesses try to tread water. What this looks like in a practical sense is little reinvestment, no effort for leadership development, systems that do not get upgraded, degrading customer service, and an inability to hire good talent.

My suggestion to these business owners is always that they sell their business before they do irreparable damage.

If you, like me, believe that a business must grow, or more accurately, must fight like heck to grow, then you need to be aware of the distinction between poor growth and good growth. What is poor growth? It comes in four different flavors:

1. Growth that outstrips your available capital
2. Growth that doesn't fit your strategy
3. Growth beyond your operating capability
4. Growth at the expense of margin

It is very possible to grow yourself broke (i.e. run out of money) even though your income statement shows good profit. Financial reporting is very necessary, but flawed. Profit does not match up in financial periods all that well with cash, particularly if you have a product business (vs. service) and/or large capital investments that get depreciated. In short, if when you sell something, you have to pay for the components before you receive payment from your customer, you can easily grow yourself broke. It has to do with the cash conversion cycle. [6] I'll illustrate with two examples from my past:

I helped grow the Kinko's organization years ago as an executive. We had a business model at the time that virtually printed money as we grew. We collected cash for products and services long before we had to pay for rent, equipment expense, supply expense, or labor. We also had virtually no finished goods or inventory. Our cash conversion cycle was approximately a *negative* 30 days. In other words, on average we received cash from our customers 30 days before we had to pay our bills. When you combine that with a healthy profit margin, you're golden!

---

6   Cash Conversion Cycle = Inventory conversation period + Receivables conversion period – Payables conversion period.

This was a result of what was at the time primarily a cash business. It was also due to the fact that we had favorable equipment leases, we were invoiced for machine usage at the end of the month and given thirty day terms, and that we were able to negotiate favorable terms on supplies and rent (usually two or three months free rent in exchange for a longer term lease). We also had enough draw that our stores became busy very quickly. Warning: If you had a negative profit margin and used these tactics, you'd basically have a Ponzi scheme!

In contrast to this, I was at one point tasked with turning around a product company with a cash conversion cycle that was at 111 days when I arrived. We had to buy our materials from Hong Kong and pay for them when they were put on the boat. When the components finally hit our warehouse we had some light assembly that took place and then we had lots of inventory. We sold to large retail chains that paid around 75 days after receiving the goods. So on average, we had to fund the sale of a product for 111 days before we were paid. If we grew rapidly, we would run out of money, *even though we had "profit" on each product that was fairly healthy.* Couple that with markdowns on obsolete products (they changed frequently) and retailers that stuck us with a high level of returns, and it was a very unhealthy business model even though we showed a profit. Our immediate challenge was to reduce our cash conversion cycle.

Real Lesson: Your business can be profitable and still run out of money, and growth can exacerbate this! Take the time to figure out what you can do to create a better cash conversion cycle.

Strategic vs. Opportunistic Growth

Opportunistic growth that doesn't fit your strategy can seem profitable in the short term and is very difficult to turn down. Here are a couple of examples:

- A solutions company that stumbles into a new product and tries to have their sales people not only be adroit problem solvers, but also product pushers. They don't do well and their customers get confused. The people hired to be "product people" (e.g. engineers) don't understand the lack of support from the solutions driven people, or why their budget is starved when they want to develop new products.

- An operationally driven company that is a low cost provider implements a high-end sales force to sell to a different, more discerning customer. The sales people push for solutions that stretch beyond the capabilities of the current operations and pretty soon G&A expense is out of control and customers are confused.

- A middle of the road restaurant tries to attract higher end customers with a face-lift of their facility and furnishings. They raise prices but still sell "average" quality food and provide less than premium service levels. Now those looking for good value and those looking for a high quality meal are both disappointed; all in the name of chasing growth.

Brands and strategies can only be stretched so far; therefore, you must be strategic about growth. If you identify a new growth opportunity—not just a new color or size or line extension, but rather something quite different—I'd like to ask you the following questions:

1. Will your current core customer appreciate this?
2. What is the financial benefit?
3. Do you have the competencies to offer this?
4. If I were going to start this new business line from scratch, would it fit your current brand or be better off under a new umbrella?
5. Will this distract you and potentially hamper your core business?

The chart below—a derivation of what is known as the Ansoff Matrix[7]—is designed to help you to think about growth opportunities. The current/current box is your current business. To expand this box you need to execute better, and if your market share is low that is likely your best option, as it is your least risky option. The further away from this box you get, the greater the change you must undertake to be successful. If you go all the way to the new product/new market box, you effectively have a start-up business.

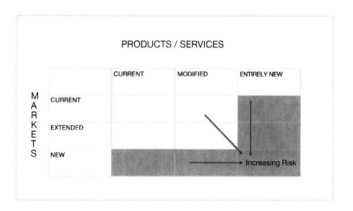

Real Lesson: If you are focused on long-term success, growth opportunities should pass not only a financial hurdle, but also a strategic one. Your brand can only stretch so far. Consider a new brand and operating model if it is too far from home (e.g. Toyota sells luxury models under the Lexus brand).

Can we do this?

Every business has one or more core competencies—a set of skills that distinguishes it from other businesses and can often be expanded to new markets. However, when stretched too far, they become diluted and sometimes lost. If McDonald's thought of one of their competencies

---

7   This dates back to 1957 and was introduced by Igor Ansoff.

as "grilling meat," they might convince themselves that they should try to introduce fillet mignon to their menu. This not only violates the strategic principle addressed above, but would also cause them to exceed their operating skills and practices.

A successful example of this is a division of a publishing company that I mentioned earlier who changed their business model from selling educational books to a solutions provider model. They knew that they could not address all of the requirements of their new model with existing competencies (e.g. editorial services), and as a result acquired new businesses and employees with existing competencies in putting on educational events and providing consulting services.

Real Lesson: If you find an opportunity that passes the financial and strategic hurdles that you've identified, but that exceeds your operating capabilities, you must decide whether you will buy or build those new capabilities.

If they are not profitable, you can't make it up in volume!

I mentioned earlier that I had been involved in turning around some struggling businesses. In one case, my first day in the company revealed that they were about to give up the ghost if there was not some fast intervention. My CFO quickly analyzed our customers and products, and discovered that we were actually losing money (on a *net* basis not *gross*—more about this next) on one of our largest customers and had been for several years! When I approached the sales manager about this, he stammered on for a minute and then said something that caused me to laugh. He said, "Yes... but it is a strategic account!"

I fired the account—and royally pissed off the account manager who had been paid commission on this revenue— and they came back a year later with renegotiated terms in a profitable fashion.

Real Lesson: In a push for growth it is easy to convince yourself of many things, but once you head down the path of growth at the expense of margin, be careful!

Financial Lesson # 4: *Think net, not gross!*

The problem with the account that I mentioned above was that while there was a small amount of positive gross margin, they had not factored in a number of other expenses. First, it was basically a consignment account; they paid us when they sold items, thus tying up large amounts of our capital sitting on their shelves. Secondly, we incurred extraordinary accounting and sales expense to service this account. In other words, much of our G&A expense could be attributed to trying to satisfy this account. My talented new CFO figured out very quickly that while the account made money from a gross margin perspective, we were actually losing money once we applied overhead.

If you were to (and you should!) accurately identify the net profit from each of your customers or customer types (i.e. not just gross margin, but after all overhead is applied), and stack rank them from highest to lowest, I am pretty confident that the graphical depiction would look like the chart below. In this case there are 20 customers. The first 11 generate all of the profit and the next 9 are net losers.

The trick is to apply all overhead to your customers. There are many categorization techniques (e.g. % of sales, four buckets, etc.), but I believe that a modified activity-based-costing process is best.[8]

What do you do with the information that you generate? Here are three simple, but not so easy, steps that should generate significant profit over time:

1. Identify the best customers' characteristics and find more of them (customers).
2. Fix or fire the worst customers.
3. Put in a "performance improvement plan" for breakeven customers.

Real Lesson: Gross margin is critical, but if you use a lot of overhead to service a customer, a customer group, an individual product, or a product line, you may be fooling yourself!

Financial Lesson # 5: *You can't cut your way to greatness!*

I've worked with a number of private equity firms, some that I admire and others that I do not. One of the characteristics of those that I do not admire is that they view businesses the way that fashion magazines view female models— the thinner the better. Worse yet, they often have many rounds of cost cutting over a short period of time. As a good friend of mine says, "If you are going to cut the tail off of a dog, don't do it an inch at a time."

An owner in a large retail business that I worked with once told me that he wanted to minimize labor as it was his largest expense line on the income statement. I told him that I thought that was foolish as

---

8   If you want some good background on this perspective, I recommend you read: Kaplan, R. and Narayaan, V.G., "Customer Profitability Measurement and Management" *Journal of Cost Management*, September/October, 2001.

"labor" was what drove delight in his customers (something they were known for) and that he should "optimize" labor rather than minimize it. Thankfully, he took my advice.

Looking at cost in a vacuum, not recognizing the benefits, and underestimating the consequences of cutting expenses all describe the actions of someone who took financial management classes, but skipped the classes on strategy and growth.

Don't get me wrong—wasting money in a business is foolish. There is a large opportunity cost in doing so. Profits propel growth initiatives, they keep people employed *in the long run*, and through the magic of the multiplier effect, profits propel our economy.

Paul Orfalea, founder of Kinko's, was notorious for roaming the mailroom to see who had used extra money to FedEx a document to headquarters because they were too late to use regular mail. At the same time, he spent millions of dollars every year on an annual meeting called "the Picnic" for thousands of people because it was a cultural linchpin. (Ironically, FedEx eventually bought Kinko's, the Picnic went away, the name Kinko's went away, and I'm guessing that they have no problem sending overnight packages to headquarters!) Paul knew that there was foolish expense and that there was good expense—even though others may not see it that way.

Real Lesson: Rather than thinking of minimizing expenses, think in terms of optimizing investment. Spend your money wisely, but think through the unintended consequences when you are about to make cuts.

Profit is important to every business. But if you want to produce a profit, you must first cultivate and care for your business. Engage your team and work together to come up with solid ideas and winning strategy. When business picks up, remember that you need to grow wisely so that you can maximize your profit in the long-term. This might require you to carefully assess your accounts, and you might even need to make some cuts, but be careful not to go overboard. Take care to invest in the future.

Chapter Review:

Listen Up: Take a long lunch and write down your assumptions and financial expectations for your business. Have a conversation with your board or an outside advisor who has no dog in the hunt. You need to get beyond, "more profit is always better" and "lower costs are always preferable."

Quick Wins: Do some homework on activity-based-costing as a method of overhead allocation and then talk to your CFO or controller about customer and product *net* profitability—all overhead accounted for. Follow the three steps outlined in the "Think net, not gross" section.

Graduate Work: If you really want your employees to think and act like owners, then you should consider treating them like owners. Open book management is not a silver bullet for all companies, but it is a very powerful tool for those with stable management and supportive ownership.

CHAPTER EIGHT

YIPPEE KI YAY—COWBOY WISDOM IN THE BUSINESS WORLD

There is nothing better than the wild, Wild West: Gun-slinging cowboys, damsels in distress, and plenty of bar-fights at the local saloon. There was lots of chaos and things could get out of hand, but there was also cowboy justice, with hard and fast sheriffs doing their best to maintain order. Sometimes, I feel that leading a business is like being a sheriff in the Wild West. You play lots of roles, wear plenty of hats, and are always looking out for the next villain riding into town to cause trouble. The competition is fierce, the obstacles are ever-present, and while I exhort you to spend time planning each week, you often just don't know what you are in for when you walk into the office.

But it is that Wild West mentality that inspired me to give you some of the best cowboy rules in the land. These rules are applicable to the Wild West of business leadership and should help to give you some great

109

clarity around how to survive in the exciting, but often chaotic, world of business leadership.

My father-in-law, a man I greatly admired, reminded me a lot of Will Rogers. He used to say things like, *"Let's mount up!"* when we were supposed to get in the car to go out, or *"Let's break camp!"* when we were done with dinner. One day I realized that all of Rogers' quips had significant business implications.

Many know Rogers only as a film star, but he was also an accomplished author, political commentator, and radio broadcaster. He was even nominated to be the governor of Oklahoma (he declined) and was appointed honorary mayor of Beverly Hills. In short, even though he is best known as a cowboy, Will Rogers was a successful businessman, which is why we can apply some of his wisdom to our current study.

For this chapter, I compiled a list of "Cowboy Rules" that can be incorporated into your leadership strategy to help you navigate the often torrential terrain that comes with being a CEO (Cowboy hat and horse not included).

Cowboy Rule # 1: *"Never kick a cow chip on a hot day"*

Perhaps like me, you've charged up a hill, shot from the hip, or quickly used an "obvious" solution only to find out that the result was smelly boots. I admit to having a bias for action and believe that executives who don't are dangerous. If you wait until you have enough information for the decision to make itself, you might be 100 percent confident, but your decision may be irrelevant. Even "Ready, Fire, Aim" is preferable to "Ready, Aim, Aim, Aim…"

However, managers often don't consider how decisions or actions will impact the rest of the organization or, even worse, the customers— ergo the phrase "unintended consequences." In business, there's no stronger evidence of this law than in compensation. Reward systems and the field of economics can explain most human behavior. How often have you seen compensation plans change to reward certain behaviors, only to eventually cause even worse problems?

Here's an example from my past: In an effort to maintain a very rapid growth rate at Kinko's (which at the time was a very successful retail company serving small businesses and home office type customers), I put in a professional sales force, led by a very bright and aggressive guy. He naturally had his people calling on Fortune 500 customers because they had large printing budgets. However, the work that came into our stores and the demands of doing high quality, high volume work stretched our systems and frayed relationships with our existing customers. We would have been better off segmenting this work and running it through closed-door production centers, but I didn't see all of the unintended consequences.

This is the terrain of "systems thinking"—a formal thought process that considers the whole system and studies the challenges of reductionism. (Remember Descartes from your high school philosophy class?) The subject is actually quite fascinating, and those who are adept in systems thinking have some very cool tools and techniques to guide decision-making.[9]

Real Lesson: How can you easily employ a bit of systems thinking in your world? Try to view decisions in the larger context. Ask, "Who or what else might this impact and how? How will they react?" Be decisive, but consider the unintended consequences of your actions. Understand relationships and pecking orders before you spout off, and think about unintended consequences before you act.

Cowboy Rule # 2: *"Never miss a good chance to shut up"*

As you rise in the ranks of an organization, you are required to talk more and to deliver inspiring, strategic messages. The unintended consequence

---

9   Peter Senge is a great author on this subject.

of talking more is that you listen less. The problem is, you can't learn a darn thing with your mouth open!

One of the challenges in a senior leadership role is to know when to talk and when to shut up. Unfortunately, we usually only shut up when we are around those who are higher in the pecking order. The challenge is that now you are at (or near) the top! This is, in many ways, a dangerous place to be: If yours is the only voice you listen to, you will get into a world of hurt.

I would like for you to do two things that at first blush may seem like opposing objectives—listen more and speak more effectively.

People who are promoted into senior management but have not had consistent opportunities for delivering leadership messages—both positive and negative—are usually not good at it. Difficult, assertive conversations as well as positive, encouraging conversations must become muscle memory before you can use them as needed. Most of us aren't skilled enough to "wing it."

I had an extremely talented CEO client who used to call me to practice his difficult conversations as well as his planned, encouraging talks to coworkers. If you saw him in action you'd wonder why because he was articulate and could think quickly on his feet. However, he understood the importance of language and tone, and knew that sometimes our intended messages got tangled up in our mouths on the way to the recipient's ears. What we think we're saying is often not heard the way we intend.

Most of us suffer through the initial challenges of delivering leadership messages and eventually do enough reps to be effective. However, with some coaching, mentoring, and practice we can learn effective communication much more quickly.

I'm a miserable golfer. I never took the time to learn it very well and, as a result, turn down offers to golf. I remember taking a lesson or two many years ago and the instructor said, "If you want to go for a beautiful walk, golf. If you want to learn how to golf, practice!" In the organizational world, delivering tough or compelling messages and having the kind, yet ferocious, conversations required to succeed can be learned on the job—but they're better learned through practice.

Real Lesson: I've gained much better results by a) getting to know people and b) learning things by asking questions rather than talking. The other day I actually had to say to a guy, "O.K., enough about you, let's talk about me!" after he droned on about himself for 30 minutes. You want to make sure that other people aren't thinking the same thing about you! When you take the opportunity to talk, take care to speak in compelling terms and occasionally take the opportunity to just shut up and listen.

Cowboy Rule # 3: *"Always drink upstream from the herd"*

Have you ever found yourself hanging around the water cooler with a bunch of cynical people who have lots to complain about but no solutions to offer? If so, then head upstream!

Optimism is a quality of an emotionally intelligent leader. Perhaps as you rose through the ranks, you've been part of a team led by someone who believed that their team was destined for great things. It's inspiring and fun, and it gives you a fighting chance to scale tall mountains. (Too much optimism, of course, is delusional. When the horse is dead, you can't will it to victory. It's time to get off and find another horse.)

There is a dangerous disease that can suck the optimism out of a team faster than The Grinch can steal presents from Whoville—cynicism. Although not the direct opposite of optimism (which is pessimism), cynicism can bog down an organization and put a good size ding in the culture. Can optimism and cynicism simultaneously exist in large quantities? I don't think so.

Having a small bit of this affliction, I appreciate the well-timed cynical comment that can lighten up a situation. For example, "Other than *that*, Mrs. Lincoln, how did you like the play?" The problem occurs when cynicism becomes embedded in an organization through its conversations, meetings, and even processes. When you start from a position of, "This ain't gonna work," or "All of my people are dopes," you're in trouble. Bart Simpson is cynical and funny, but no one would follow him into battle.

Cynicism robs people of energy. Why show enthusiasm for a new product, customer, or idea when the room will just shoot it down? Cynicism also destroys innovation. If my ideas have to get through Calvin Curmudgeon to see the light of day, I'll quit trying (or just quit). Cynics don't see failure as a necessary step to success; they see it as predictive … of everything!

Cynics also like to hang out together; they find energy in wallowing in negative thought. Interestingly, however, they rarely offer solutions and are not good members of problem solving teams, as they just want to bring up more problems. I'll bet there aren't too many cynics in Apple's product development organization. Cynics can't stand to be around positive, optimistic people. It wears them out. They cringe when they hear words such as "Outstanding!" and "Great job!" because they believe good things happen to those who are lucky, not good.

Real Lesson: As Smokey the Bear said, "Only you can prevent forest fires!" As the CEO, only you can prevent cynicism. Don't get caught up in the negative groupthink of the herd and for goodness sake, don't foster it! Optimism works, and it's infectious!

Cowboy Rule # 4: *"Good judgment comes from experience, and a lot of that comes from bad judgment"*

I love getting older! Okay, not all elements. My knees hurt from the five surgeries I've had and I sometimes forget my wife's name—but age brings experience and perhaps a reduced level of concern about what others think. I don't blush as often as I used to when I say, "I don't know." I believe that my effectiveness is much higher when I quit worrying about having all of the answers.

Making mistakes and being exposed (vulnerable is another great word) is uncomfortable at first, but it is much more genuine than being a pretender. Do you really like working with Mr. Perfect who never admits defeat, or that he doesn't know something?

With a German mother—a personality type that wants to know all of the details, desires to always make the right decision, and holds a healthy fear of failure—I have had to fight the desire to control all situations. Being exposed and giving up control does not come naturally. However, to move forward, you need to let go of the dead weight.

Running the Rolex watch factory requires extreme control and little ambiguity. However, in most business situations, regardless of your role, admitting when you are stuck and sharing leadership with other group members can be very liberating, and much more effective than shooting for perfection. You may have heard, "It's about success, not perfection." Many people in a position of leadership—not all of who are really "leaders"—would benefit from being more exposed. You really don't engender trust in others when you always have shields up. "Never let them see you sweat" might be good advice if you compete in mixed martial arts cage fighting, but it is really pretty naïve and ineffective in business.

Ironically, being exposed requires you to be fearless. Have you noticed that some people are able to be completely honest in most situations, while others fret over the consequences? A good friend explained a work situation to me and wondered if he was being too honest with his boss. Being fearless can lead to unemployment, but constantly biting your tongue only leads to misery.

A word of caution: Being exposed and fearless requires that you are interacting with emotionally intelligent people. And if you aren't, why not? I learned early in my career that it is best to consider yourself self-employed at all times. While this attitude can lead to finding yourself out of a job if you work for a jerk (or a board of jerks), I wouldn't do it any other way.

Real Lesson: It's hard to make a case for intentionally making mistakes, but I've observed that true leaders are not afraid of making mistakes, and that failing fast is a good skill set. An old boss from many years ago said, *"You'll never get rich running scared! Make some mistakes!"*

Cowboy Rule # 5: *"If you're riding ahead of the herd, take a look back every now and then to make sure it's still there"*

I recently met with a very bright CEO who was a great strategic thinker. He was smart as a whip, had undergraduate and graduate degrees from world-class schools, and was very articulate.

As I started to interact with his partner and some of the senior leaders in the company, it became clear that this CEO was riding way ahead of the herd and couldn't figure out why they weren't keeping up. In fact, most of the leaders hoped that this guy would just ride over the horizon so that they didn't have to try to follow him anymore.

In business, the whole team needs to get across the goal line at the same time. He had to slow down and play the game as a team sport rather than as a solo activity. (As you might guess, he also needed to learn to listen better and have more self-awareness.) Brilliant thoughts that go unexecuted don't lead to success.

I was fortunate some years ago to be able to spend a good deal of time with the senior executive of one of the largest companies in the world. He was wicked smart, didn't suffer fools—he scared the hell out of most people—and like the previous example, was often many steps ahead of the team. However, this executive listened to criticism (as long as someone was brave enough to approach him). He employed a more junior executive to follow him around and take notes. At the end of every day, the junior executive would help this brilliant senior executive prioritize, recap, and reposition his thoughts so that the "mere mortals" working for him would understand and be able to execute what were usually brilliant ideas.

Real Lesson: You must frequently check for understanding with your people. Ask them to feed back to you what they have heard. If it is not what you intended, it is probably not their fault, but rather something that you need to refine or articulate in a different fashion. A coach, mentor, or trusted colleague can help with this.

Cowboy Rule # 6: *"If you find yourself in a hole, stop digging"*

Fundamental attribution error says that when we see others with a problem, we assume that they are flawed. When we have a problem ourselves, we tend to blame the environment. Let's say you're running a company (or division) and your results stink. Do you dig faster? Or do you think about digging elsewhere? It's not always an easy decision. Is it you or the environment?

I could make the case that many great ideas have been lost in business for lack of perseverance. We love stories of toil and struggle with happy endings. I happen to live in Boulder, Colorado, and we are home to quite a few of the early craft brewing companies (that's beer, for the uninitiated) in the country. Most all have stories of long hours, and weeks, and years of schlepping a case or two of beer around in their Volkswagen van trying to break into a tight market controlled by Budweiser or Coors, only to eventually become successful and wealthy.

Unfortunately, for each of those stories, there are quite a few more depicting a bright industrious individual, whether company founder or hired gun, who cannot let go of a bad idea and ends up in a very large hole as a result, either financially or career wise.

Real Lesson: You need to have a group of advisors, as well as a process for reflection, that allows you to see things from different perspectives.

Ignoring the advice of markets, customers, close advisors, and the voice of reason could be a sign that you are a driven entrepreneur, but it most likely means that you are stubborn beyond reason.

Cowboy Rule # 7: *"There are three kinds of men: The ones that learn by reading, the few who learn by observation, and the rest of them have to pee on the electric fence and find out for themselves"*

A few years ago, some friends and I were skiing in Whistler, British Columbia. We watched a young Australian guy named Angus jump off a very large rock with a flat landing spot—a big mistake, as it tends to make you go splat. (I know his name because I helped him collect his gear and limbs.) We then watched his three buddies all do the same thing with identical results. I guess the 4th guy must have been the dumbest. Experiential learning is great, but there is a lot to be learned from observation (and it is much less painful).

This is a close cousin to the rule about digging a deep hole. My advice is to dig a lot of holes, but don't let them get too deep.

I am amazed when I watch some executives do things that have proven to be foolish. They would include:

- Hoping without planning
- Poor pay and incentive practices
- Refusing to consider risk in their business model (e.g. concentration issues)
- No attention to the changing business environment around them
- Keeping weak team members
- Expecting loyalty without fostering engagement and showing appreciation

We could make this a long list. I'm sure that I had some significant violations when I was in senior roles as well. However, there is no good excuse for not studying good business practices.

Benchmarking is overrated, and in fact can be dangerous. You need to think for yourself, but no one has yet been able to defy gravity, live forever, or run a business without cash flow. You won't either.

Real Lesson: You must bring your original ideas to your work, but take the time to observe the world around you by reading the business news, talking with other business executives, and learning from others who have gone before you.

Life is never boring in the wild, Wild West. There are lots of lessons to be learned along the dusty road to success. You are dealt some tricky hands as a leader, and chances are you will often get some mud on your boots, but just remember that you deserve to kick your feet up and relax every now and then. And don't forget about the cowboy wisdom!

Chapter Review:

Listen Up: Have a sense of humor! Leading others is hard work and it'll be much more fun if you laugh! Make work fun for your team. Don't assume that they all have the same sense of humor, but rather that they all like to laugh. My experience is that teams that laugh together are more committed.

Quick Wins: There is an old saying that you need to work "on" your business as well as "in" it. Part of what I am trying to get you to do is to think about what you are doing rather than just reverting to past practice. You need to schedule some time each week to be reflective. The process is enhanced if you can have some dialogue with a coach or a colleague.

Graduate Work: Write your own rules. Call them "[Insert Your Name Here]'s Rules for Prosperity, Profit and Fun." Seriously, if you wrote your top 10 business or leadership rules every year, I believe that you would attain heightened clarity. Better yet, share them with your team and ask them for feedback—and then shut up! (See Cowboy Rule Number Two!)

CHAPTER NINE

IT'S CALLED LEADING, NOT PRESIDING—LEADERSHIP COMES WITH OBLIGATIONS

After years of breathing their own exhaust, many CEOs develop a sense of entitlement. Everyone wants to please them, and few dare speak the truth to them, especially when the news is painful. CEOs are paid handsomely and can wield significant power with the stroke of a pen or key. Emotionally intelligent CEOs, however, realize that they are not only somewhat special, but also that they have significant obligations and duties along with the accouterments of the office. As a CEO, you are responsible for people's livelihood, shareholder returns and, I would argue, for the continuity of capitalism and commerce. Feeling stressed yet?

If you think of leadership as a choice, not a rank, (or as an obligation to be great, not a right) you'll be a far better CEO. Positional authority doesn't make you a great leader, but creating a great environment for your people to prosper so that they can satisfy your customers absolutely does.

In this chapter, I will share what I believe to be the seven most important obligations that are on your shoulders as a CEO. If you take these seriously, then I believe that I can help you balance your rights with your obligations. (When you believe that your rights exceed your obligations, you'll likely encounter one or all of the following: a visit from the enforcement division of the SEC, a dramatic spike in the turnover of your best employees, or your spouse heading for the door.) Finding a balance between the two is crucial for long-term success.

Obligation # 1: *Procreate*

You may recall that 'Mantra #1' from the first chapter on leadership was that successful executives are not nice. Kind, yes, but not nice. Some time ago I served on a board of directors and we were in executive session preparing for a review with the CEO. This CEO had a wonderful personality and a good team that loved him. However, he was not effectively dealing with the tough decisions and problems in front of him. At one point, the chairman said, "He's not really leading, he's just presiding!" I've always remembered that quip because it was spot-on and described other CEOs that I have interacted with. They are what I call "chocolate bunnies." They are frauds.

I recently had coffee with a fraud. He looked good, smelled good, dropped names, and used buzzwords like a pro. However, he was a chocolate bunny—sweet on the outside and hollow on the inside. These characters avoid tough decisions and can deflect blame like a superhero deflects bullets. All fluff and no stuff, they add no value to organizations.

But how do chocolate bunnies evolve? I believe they grow up in organizations with weak leadership, meaning they were never really held accountable for their actions and results. Perhaps they're even "mentored" by someone who has mastered the art of "nonstick" and is unwittingly passing their skills on to the next generation of bunnies.

When this happens to young businesspeople, they grow old in age, but do not grow any real skills. They are frauds, and it's only partially their fault. When they eventually get into a healthy organization that requires true performance, accountability and emotional intelligence, they fail every time. They often make great strides early on because they're gregarious and look good; but once uncovered, they nervously jump from job to job looking for the sanctuary of their early career when being a good guy was enough.

A retired Marine once told me that the most important job of the Marines is to create other Marines. They seek out their best and make them recruiters and drill instructors. I believe that one of the most important jobs of a CEO is to create other leaders.

So how do you cultivate effective leaders and avoid creating chocolate bunnies? Here are five rules that should help:

1. **Avoid the "nice versus kind" trap.** It's nice to avoid conflict and only give people positive feedback, but it's not kind. Real leaders speak the truth and take the long-term view.

2. **Fire faster.** Gosh, that doesn't sound nice, does it? I have yet to meet the leader who says that he or she has been too quick to pull the trigger on nonperformers. My belief is that those who violate your values should be the first to go. Even high performers who violate your values and culture need to be shown the door. You want a company full of ethical, high performance people that are fully engaged and respectful to the big picture.

3. **Focus on development.** Provide support (and funding) for your people to develop themselves professionally, and insist that

they do so. Both components are necessary: the tools and a bit
of a push.

4. **Focus on value.** How does each person on your team add value
   to the organization? Ask them. If they don't add value but they
   have talent, help them re-create their job. No good person
   wants to come to work and not add value!

5. **Plan and review.** People who execute a meaningful plan with
   specific objectives tied to the organization's global strategy
   cannot turn into chocolate bunnies. The more frequent
   the feedback, the better! The best teams that I work with
   communicate frequently.

Real Lesson: Holding people accountable does not make you a
"mean" manager; it creates others who can step up when required
and bring more value to the team. Don't create chocolate bunnies
and for goodness sake, don't become one yourself! Create a tracking
mechanism for your up-and-coming leaders with clearly identified
development plans.

Obligation # 2: *Unchain and engage your people*
As my wife tells me when I get self-absorbed, "It's really not all about
you!" When you reach the top of the pyramid in your company—
whether you are the owner or a hired gun—it's not really all about
you either!

If business were as easy as rowing a boat, perhaps you could chain
your people to their oars like galley slaves on a ship from *Ben Hur*, pound
a rhythmic drum, and reach your destination. I've met "leaders" who
metaphorically treat their people this way. They were not optimizing
their profit potential, not servicing their customers like they should,
had a high rate of turnover, and generally took enjoyment away from

their employees during their work hours. That is a bad way to run a business—even if you believe that you have a right to do so.

As CEO, getting your team to joyfully pull on the oars is one of your biggest challenges; but I'd prefer that you think about it as an opportunity. You have the opportunity to do good work, produce a healthy profit, and help create enjoyment in the workplace. Where else can you find a job like that?

Engaging the hands and minds of your coworkers is most often achieved by focusing on their hearts. I'm not a particularly "mushy" guy, so I won't get all romantic, but instead will appeal to the desire that brought you to buy this book—being a successful leader.

What is engagement? When people joyfully participate in the success of the company, they are engaged. How does this happen? It happens when a company joyfully participates in the success of its employees. Asking for loyalty and hard work from your employees without allowing them to use their minds along with their hands is folly.

If you search, you'll find many studies that equate employee engagement to better results. I'm not vouching for their efficacy, as you can easily make studies of soft skills say pretty much whatever you want. I have a better measure of success—I've seen it with my own eyes many times. If you want to feel better about my "proof," you can call it empirical evidence or say it achieves face validity. (By this point in the book, you either believe me, or you don't!)

The following six steps will help effectively engage your employees:

1. **Allow your team to help craft their own work.** You might, if so inclined, have them assist in developing a vision or strategy; but at very least, let them come up with the ideas as to how to execute the strategy and add value to the firm. Insist that they do so!

2. **Communicate frequently,** and by this I mean listen as much as you speak. Give them feedback and take some of your own. Employees who do not align with the values, vision and strategy that you are consistently espousing will often self-select out of the company, while those who are aligned will gain enthusiasm through the communication, and you'll gain insight from the interaction.

3. **Have fun!** I'm serious! You need to make work an enjoyable place to be (even if you run a virtual company), so that people will want to be there. Remember, you want commitment, not just compliance.

4. **Commit to a meritocracy.** Treat everyone with respect, but don't put everyone in charge. Reward and promote the best performers. "Fairness" (i.e. treating and rewarding everyone the same) will just piss off your best employees—the ones that you really need engaged! Remember, no chocolate bunnies!

5. **Provide your people with development opportunities.** If they run faster and jump higher, they develop a sense of pride and the firm wins too.

6. **Share the fruits of success.** Whether you go "all the way to bright" and put in a profit sharing program with open book management, or use a more scaled back version, your people will have great appreciation if you share the gains.

Real Lesson: If you follow these six steps, you'll get most everyone rowing in the same direction with a good deal of intensity—no drum or chains required!

Obligation # 3: *Sharpen your own saw*

It is a tremendous achievement to get to the C-suite! When you get there, you should feel a sense of well-deserved pride. The dirty little secret that

I'd like to share with those of you who are not yet there is that even the most experienced CEOs question their abilities, have momentary lapses of confidence, and occasionally doubt their skills. Only the emotionally intelligent ones, however, will admit this.

There is a difference between confidence and hubris. You need to develop one and avoid the other. One is rewarded and the other punished. Confidence may be one of the most important characteristics you need as a leader.

Building and maintaining confidence is only one reason that you need to allocate time and energy to sharpening your saw. As noted earlier, the amount of change going on is dizzyingly fast. If you don't keep up, your organization, your financial results, and your people will suffer.

The image of the wise old CEO who has all of the answers is not healthy. You need only to look at some of the past and current world leaders to realize that wisdom does not always correlate with position, and that self-development should not stop just because you have reached a high level. The best athletes in the world all have coaches and they must work to continually improve, or they are dropped from the team. Peyton Manning, one of the best quarterbacks of all time, still spends lots of time studying the game and reviewing previous plays from the bench.

I believe that leadership development is primarily self-development. I've yet to see a leader who has been spoon-fed courses throughout his career make it to the top. All of the wonderful leaders that I have worked with have taken it upon themselves to create a plan for their own development and to seek out new opportunities to learn. There are always new heights we can reach, if only we work and study hard.

My best clients are constantly looking for new avenues to improve themselves through both formal and informal means. Some of the vehicles available to you are:

- Executive programs at universities
- Mastermind groups of your peers
- Working with a coach
- Networking with successful leaders
- Joining boards of directors in other industries
- Voracious reading
- Getting feedback on the gaps in your skills and working on them
- Putting yourself into new situations
- Teaching either in a university setting or your own company

My observation is that top-down leadership development programs in companies where the senior leaders do not appear to be doing anything to better themselves is pretty much a waste of time. Setting a good example means doing it in a visible way, and it will very likely set the organization on the right track.

Real Lesson: Leaders who are naturally curious and focused on self-improvement have a better chance of long-term success vs. those who are cemented into a narrow skill set and mode of operation.

Obligation # 4: *Make a profit*

"Profit is not the explanation, cause, or rationale of business behavior and business decisions, but the test of the validity."
—Peter Drucker

As CEO, you don't get credit for just trying hard. Earlier in your career, you may have been rewarded for good process and good effort. As CEO, effort and process are still very important, but they won't save you from bad financial results. If you are not ready for that reality, don't try to get there. As a current Zach Brown Band song says, "heavy is the head that wears the crown."

The CEO's desk is where strategy and execution collide. One without the other won't cut it. This, in my mind, is the primary reason that people say, "it is lonely at the top." The CEO is the one person in the organization who has to ensure that the boat is going in the right direction and that everyone is rowing hard.

As the quote from Drucker indicates, the financial results you achieve are merely a test of your strategy and your ability to execute. (However, luck—both good and bad—can play a role as well. As I said, life's not fair!)

Here again, I am not advocating for maximizing short-term profit, but rather optimizing for the long-term. Society only benefits when companies produce a profit. A failed company means lost jobs, dissatisfied customers, and losses for investors.

Real Lesson: Capitalism is a moral system and I believe that as business people, we have a duty to ensure its continuation. Getting everyone to the same starting line is the job, in great measure, of families and the government. Rewarding those who work hardest and smartest with disproportionate rewards is the duty of capitalism, and with it all boats rise!

Obligation # 5: *Think deeply*

Most, if not all, of the people in a company outside of the CEO have a functional responsibility and do not see the whole picture. While I have in earlier sections tried to get you to allow your people to be engaged and think like owners, here I will say that they will never get *all* the way there. Only when you get to the very top do you see the entire mountain.

Not long ago, I spoke to a recently promoted CEO who for several years previous had been the CFO. He shared with me that the first few weeks were exhilarating, but he also expressed surprise at how the view was much different even though his office had been figuratively and literally next door to the CEO's prior to his promotion. He was challenged with some vexing issues and his second weekend in his new role found him in the office, alone, on a Saturday. He said he sat at his desk for most of the day just thinking and developing some much needed clarity.

By the time that you are in the top chair in the office, you have many admirers and perhaps many detractors; they all want a piece of your calendar and you are forced, in great measure, to do your job in 15 minute increments. Get used to it. With that said, you need to occasionally change your environment, get some alone time, and think deeply. I used to find this time on Saturday morning in the office, on my road bike on a long solo ride, or sometimes by having a deep conversation with a trusted colleague. (I was an executive before executive coaches were a viable option.)

Real Lesson: Regardless of how you do it, you need to peel back the onion on your business and get beyond the fire drills in order to get some clarity. This will help to see your opportunities and challenges more clearly. You must spend less time "doing" and more time thinking.

Obligation # 6: *Create clarity from chaos*

Whether you love them or hate them, Ronald Reagan and Bill Clinton had something in common that, in my opinion, set them apart from other leaders: They could communicate about complex issues in a wonderfully simple way. Chaos may have been all around them, but when they hit the stage they had wrung out the complexity of an issue and presented a cogent picture of what they wanted us to see. Great CEOs must learn to do this as well, whether we are talking about strategic direction, implementing change, or making tough decisions. There are three steps to follow that will help you create clarity from chaos:

1. **Decide what information is relevant.** This is not easy. You must learn to screen out lots of data and choose what to pay attention to. However, as you learn to ignore the noise, be careful that you don't inadvertently become deaf to certain sources or points of view. This is a delicate dance!

2. **Synthesize this data into critical themes or issues.** It helps me to write these out, but I know others who can visualize them—even turn them into pictures in their mind. When you observe great leaders at work, they can take what appears to be unrelated data points and turn them into logic.

3. **Develop clear messages** *that appeal to your audience.* Learn to look at things from their perspective. Leadership is about using your team to get to the finish line, not just getting there yourself.

It is perfectly acceptable to be open, honest and vulnerable with your team and to admit when you don't have an answer. However, they will be looking to you for clarity once you've had adequate time to digest an issue. You don't have to have all of the answers, but you do have to turn on the lights for your people so that they can see where you are taking them.

Real Lesson: The business world will always be chaotic. It is necessary for you, as CEO, to learn how to create clarity from chaos. If the President of the United States, who has the most complex work environment and most difficult job in the world, can provide clarity, can't you?

Obligation # 7: *Create a safe and trusting environment*

Combat is the last place you would think that you would find a safe, trusting environment, but if you talk to a Marine who has been in that situation, he will likely tell you that he was secure in believing that his fire team or platoon had his back. They may not have been best friends, and perhaps wouldn't even socialize in a peaceful situation, but they would risk their lives for each other in combat.

One of the reasons that combat veterans struggle when they leave the military and return to civilian life is that they don't have the same level of trust and safety that they had in the military. I saw this with my son, a combat veteran, when he returned from Iraq.

Business is a bit like combat. Others want to do you harm. Unfortunately, it is not always just your competitors that want to harm you, but sometimes your own coworkers or team members. Author Simon Sinek points out that in the military they give medals to people who sacrifice themselves so that others may gain, and yet too often in business, we give large bonuses to people who sacrifice others so that they may gain. This is not great leadership—it is merely selfish behavior.

I don't believe that a company has the same purpose as an animal shelter or a hospital ward; you can't help them all, and trying to please and save everyone is not feasible. However, when you create a safe, trusting environment that rewards true performance (for the good of the company, not the individual) you'll create one hell of a team, and great teams create great things. I know this because I have seen it over and over.

You create safety and trust by being transparent, by being true to your word, by getting rid of any chocolate bunnies that make their way into the company, and by taking good care of your people.

Real Lesson: Think about situations where you felt safe; perhaps with your family, perhaps when you worked for a great boss, perhaps in a group of friends. Create that feeling for your team, and you'll get great results.

If you haven't figured it out already, being a leader carries huge responsibilities! You have to be ready to put in the hard work required as a senior executive. (Are you still sure you want to do this?) Luckily, this chapter has made your job a little easier by providing you with the seven critical obligations you will face when you sit in the corner office. Take these to heart, and use that intelligence of yours to figure out how to deliver.

Chapter Review:

Listen Up: I've provided you a list of obligations that I believe you must own when you get to the C-suite. Create your own list, write it down and review it quarterly.

Quick Wins: Schedule a day next week to go somewhere and think about your company and the role you play within in. Go back to chapter two and revisit the three questions that I pose in the beginning of the chapter to help determine your role.

Graduate Work: Define what success looks like for you, incorporating your career, family and society. I want you to have a healthy balance sheet and income statement, but there is a lot more to life than that! Do this annually and share it with someone who listens well and will push back when appropriate.

CHAPTER TEN

BALANCING FOR BIG SHOTS

T o this point, the focus of this book has exclusively been on how to be a successful leader through leading others to action. We have journeyed through resources and tools any new or well-experienced leader can implement into his or her company to optimize and elevate the decision-making process. We all live in the consistent state of enormous desire to be fantastic leaders who lead people that want to follow us. Leadership is widely discussed, but few people can actually succeed as great leaders. It is not about merely making the most of their time, as respected leaders who are healthy—both mentally and physically—also welcome, and preach to their teams, the value of balance.

Who really wants to follow a leader who requires time in the office in lieu of time with his or her family?

What type of team will you create if you value sacrificing family, friends, and balance for work, work and more work?

And what will the overwhelming attitude be if you expect your team to view your needs as tantamount to their personal needs and the needs of their families?

In short, you will be an unsuccessful leader and you will create an environment that is poisoned with unhappiness and riddled with resentment. Thus, this book ends with quite possibly the most important lesson I could offer: a lesson in balancing for the big shots.

Finding Balance

Paul stabbed his thumb and two index fingers into the palm of his other hand. This wasn't the first time we'd heard this speech. In fact, we had heard the "tripod" speech a hundred times. Paul was the founder of Kinko's and he developed a philosophy centered on the notion of balance—which occurred when you formed a stable tripod consisting of work, love and play. If one leg was missing or shorter than the others, the tripod would be unstable or topple over. While I personally heard the story time and time again, it wasn't until I began the process of writing this book that I took the time to memorialize my thoughts on the importance of balance.

Working with my clients on a daily basis, we often find that balance is one of the most difficult goals for any leader to reach. In fact, I've yet to work with a CEO who doesn't have issues with balancing their work demands with those of family, friends, exercise, or anything else for that matter. As a leader, you probably have many of the same concerns and issues.

Thus, I'd like to finish this book with some thoughts for you regarding exactly how you can, *to the best of your ability*, create balance in your life. Keep in mind that just like deciding to be a leader, how you balance your priorities is the opportunity to make an informed decision, not create a problem.

Early in my career, I read a quote from a successful CEO. He believed he had a 20% advantage over his competitors. "I work Saturdays," he said. Sounds good in theory and there is some truth involved, but it really all depends upon how you define success. During my own years of heavy lifting, I worked very long hours and traveled most every week. At the time, I also had four young children. If my stool had four legs rather than three (the fourth being family), I would have flunked Paul's test.

I believed (and still do) that my position and role demanded a certain amount of time from me to do it correctly. This was not easy for my wife and family as an entirety, and I wished that I could help with homework more often and get to more soccer practices, but I also acknowledge that I did the best I could with the information that I had at the time. Working long hours was the decision that I made at that point in my life. And it didn't always have to be that way. Like most of us, I ultimately had a decision on how to balance my time. The same is true for you. No matter how you cut it, the decision is inevitably and ultimately yours.

There is no easy answer to the challenge of balance, so if you are looking for a silver bullet, you won't find it here (or anywhere for that matter). The fact that you will likely struggle with balance is a good thing. If you are not a bit torn as to where your loyalties lie at any given moment, then you were likely born unbalanced.

However, I have learned that there are some ways to ameliorate the challenges of being a big shot while simultaneously welcoming in a work and non-work balance. I learned many of these lessons from my clients, as I helped them forge a path through this uncharted territory.

So, the perspective that I offer has three elements:

1. Mindset
2. Values
3. A healthy dose of selfishness

The Mindset of a Balanced (relatively…) Big Shot

I talked about the need to take a long-term view of your business. However, I believe you have to do the same thing with your life. As Mickey Mantle said, "If I knew I was going to live this long, I would have taken better care of myself."

I sat next to a CEO on an airplane as I was writing this book. I learned she was also a relatively young mother. She was heading to Los Angeles for the week on business. Shortly after we spoke about her business, she showed me a picture of her young children. She had convinced her mother to move in with her family so that someone she trusted could care for her children. Smart move on her part wasn't it? I asked how she balanced work with her kids. Her response: "I have a long-term view. While I am working a lot right now, I plan to back off when we get to a certain level of business. I also take my kids on trips when I can, work from home when the opportunity arises, and work plenty after they go to sleep."

Without a long-term view, you might sacrifice your marriage, your relationship with your children, and your health to *attempt* to achieve slightly better results. Whether or not more time at work is really an advantage is debatable. A friend who is a long time CEO said that he developed a mental picture of his wife leaving him and walking out the door with his children. He would conjure up that horrific image when he felt he was a bit too wrapped up in work. While I might suggest a more positive picture, it worked for him. The notion of losing the most important thing in his own life was motivation enough to consistently take a step back and evaluate and reassess how balance looked to him.

Does this mean that you can knock off at 5:00 everyday, never work weekends and expect marital bliss over the duration of your entire career? Hardly! But it does mean that you'll go through periods in your work life where you have to sacrifice one thing for another. The goals should always be to shoot for success, not perfection. Just like you might look at a three to five year horizon for strategy in your company, I suggest that you look out three to five years in your life. To do that, begin by asking questions like:

- What do I want to achieve?
- What will these achievements look like?
- What will it take to get me there?
- What compromises am I *unwilling* to make?

Once you answer these questions, you can swiftly begin to determine exactly what your five-year plan looks like.

Real Lesson: One weekend many years ago, my father-in-law helped me build a fence in the backyard of our first home. As I mentioned earlier, this guy was one of my heroes. A World War II Veteran and Colonel in the Air Force, he flew many missions as a navigator bomber in Europe, eventually going on to become an executive in an insurance company. He went to church most every day, but swore like a sailor. We were talking about work and I was telling him how I was frustrated that I had not moved up the ladder more quickly. He responded, "What the hell is your hurry? You've got your whole life to worry about that." It was in that moment that I strived to ensure I always took the long-term view with my career.

It is through constant assessment and evaluation that you can identify the exact level of balance you maintain in your life, and if you actually need to readjust.

Make Your Values Explicit

The second element in my plan to help you create more balance within your life is assessing and understanding your values. So how do you decide what will get attention? What compromises will you make when you say "no?" One of the easiest tools I use with clients to facilitate this discussion is below. I refer to it as the values identification exercise. Take a look at the chart to help you determine your values.

Values Identification Exercise
1. Pick 10 values that are important to you (feel free to add others)
2. Reduce the list to the five that are most important
3. Reduce the list of five to three
4. Reflection: Are your actions consistent with your values? (Ask others)

Accomplishment

Advancement (career)

Adventure

Authority

Close relationships

Collaborationv

Community

Competence

Competition

Cooperation

Country

Creativity

Decisiveness

Democracy

Discretionary time

Ecological awareness

Economic security

Education

Effectiveness

Efficiency

Ethical practice

Excellence

Excitement

Fame

Family

Financial gain

Freedom

Friendships

Helping others

Honesty

Humor

Independence

Influencing others

Integrity

Job satisfaction

Knowledge

Leadership

Leading others   Location   (where you live)

Loyalty

Meaningful work

Money

Nature	Security
Order	Self-respect
Personal development	Serenity
Physical challenge	Sophistication
Pleasure	Stability
Power	Status
Privacy	Truth
Public service	Trust
Quality	Wealth
Quality relationships	Wisdom
Recognition	Variety
Religion	Work under pressure
Reputation	Work with others
Responsibility	Working alone
Risk taking	Others?

I use this tool with all of my coaching clients. Some tell me that they complete it in just a few minutes. Some tell me it pushed them to the brink for hours. Regardless, it is the fourth question that should cause you to pause and reflect upon exactly how much balance you have in your life. If the way you are spending your time is inconsistent with your values, then you're headed for trouble.

One of the things that makes me most proud of my children is that they are living lives that are consistent with their values. The one who most values nature and privacy works in the Tetons. The one who most values ecological awareness and responsibility is an environmental engineer. The one who most values beauty and creativity is an artist. The one who values loyalty and physical challenge started his career in the Marines.

If you thought that you wanted to be a CEO and your top three values are privacy, serenity, and working alone, I'd suggest that you pursue another career. I am less concerned about exactly what your values are, but rather, I want to focus you on the notion that you should maintain values, identify with them, and spend your time (personal and professional) aligning your life with them.

Real Lesson: Take the time to do an annual review for yourself, including the values exercise above as part of that review. Can you better align your activities with your values?

Selfishness has a Bad Rep...

The final element of securing balance within your life is understanding that selfishness is not always a bad trait. In fact, there are times when you absolutely have to make selfish decisions. Did you know that Winston Churchill took a nap each and everyday while bombs were falling in London during WWII? Applying this habit, a friend of mine who runs a large, very successful law firm does the same thing. Who says it has to be all about billable hours? Sometimes it is about finding balance and alignment.

Just like the phrase "put your oxygen mask on first before assisting others," you need to take care of yourself if you are going to be an effective CEO. At one point in my life, I quit a big job with thousands of employees. I decided to take a break and skied for 45 days that winter, while also taking my wife and kids to Ireland. After completing my break from work, I realized that my office phone had quit ringing—as though someone had actually unplugged it; this is the reverse of what you experience as a CEO. The higher that you go in an organization, the more people want of you. But the time I took for myself was integral to recharge and rebalance, as I had determined I was quickly losing myself. By taking that personal time, I could continue to lead at a high level.

I believe that giving of one's self to help others is noble and I greatly admire people who do so. I also believe that if you don't carve out some free time for family, fun and exercise, you'll not be as effective in the long run. You'll eventually burn out and not be able to serve anyone at a high level.

Within my own career, I was able to mix my work with my personal time. As a CEO, it is nearly impossible to separate your work life from your personal life, since we only have one life. If you work in a culture (or would like to build one as such) that allows for flexibility, I suggest that you optimize your time by stopping at the cleaners on the way to lunch, exercising when you feel like it, working after the kids are in bed, taking your spouse on business trips and tack on a day or two for fun, and take a creative attitude to find the all so crucial balance. Furthermore, impart this attitude and practice into your business to show your employees that you not only make work/life balance a priority, but also hope they do as well.

As a CEO, if you are not healthy and able to expertly apply the lessons that you have learned here and elsewhere, you are shortchanging yourself, your shareholders and, most importantly, your family. This means that you have to set boundaries. Within each of our lives, these boundaries may differ. But to get you started, here are a few that have worked for me and my clients:

1. Block out "no appointment" times on your calendar and don't let your assistant violate them. Leave the office if you must to accomplish this goal.

2. If you just put in two consecutive 18-hour days, enjoy a long morning to read the paper and talk to the kids.

3. When you are the CEO, it isn't easy to completely shut down on vacations. But how bad is working poolside? When you get back from vacation, take a day at home to catch up on all of the communication that has backed up while you are away. Then when you get back into the office, you'll be ready to go.

4. In truth, you don't need to be constantly available. If you are answering calls on a bike ride, you're cheating yourself of part of the benefit. Throw your mobile phone into a drawer once in awhile.

5. Make sure that you talk to your family or significant other about your three to five year career plans, and discuss how you will balance your work time and family time. Keeping it a secret doesn't help.

6. If you feel a great deal of guilt, do something about it. If you are guilty about how much you worked in the past, forgive yourself. You did the best with what you knew at the time.

7. You'll have to set some boundaries with your family as well as your coworkers.

8. A great executive assistant can make you much more effective, eliminate non-productive time from your schedule and, if you give your assistant permission, observe your balance and offer clear and honest feedback.

9. Put showers and a gym in your work environment. A CEO I know is also a Crossfit enthusiast and he has a Crossfit box (gym) complete with instructors on-site. Remember, the Pope put a swimming pool in his summer residence because he liked to swim.

(The Last) Real Lesson: Balance is often where good leaders become great leaders. The reality is that you can only lead as good as you feel and as happy as you are. Balance was the most natural place to finish because I don't just want you to be a successful CEO; I also want you to have a great life. There is a lot more to life than work, and if you decide to plan and execute the other important levers of your world as well as you do with your business goals, you'll be kicking up your heels rather than kicking warm cow chips!

3, 2, 1, Go!

I learned more about consulting from Alan Weiss than from anyone else. He is a brilliant guy and has a simple but brilliant message that he frequently shares: If you improve your business (or yourself) by just 1% per day, in only 70 days, you'll be twice as good. The reason that I chose to share all of the Real Lessons and Chapter Reviews in this book—aside from an attempt to create actionable clarity—was so that you can get a 1% lesson that you can implement tomorrow, the next day, and perhaps the next 68 days. By then, you'll be twice as good!

In addition to the actionable items, this book has provided you with a fortune of applicable and effective information. I designed it in way that will allow you to return to certain chapters or sections again and again if needed. Whether you want to review *The Seven Mantras of Success* or *The Five Levers of Success*, you can easily locate what you are seeking.

As you know, time is one of your most valuable resources, and I am confident that reading this book will prove to be a wise investment of your time. It may be that you adopt the OAR strategy, identify your objectives, take more confirming or corrective action, increase velocity, or adopt open book management. Heck, you might even try being more vulnerable and start engaging your people, thereby strengthening your company culture!

Or, perhaps you just stop being so nice and try kindness for a change, or maybe you remember to shut up and listen more often—whatever your take away, hopefully you have at least learned never to kick a cow chip on a hot day!

If you climb in the saddle, be ready for the ride!
Yippie ki yay!

ABOUT THE AUTHOR

Todd Ordal leverages his rich leadership background to help CEOs and other senior executives lead better, profit more or sleep soundly—usually without narcotics! He has led teams as large as 7,000, has worked as a CEO in multiple industries and served on many boards of directors.

Todd is married with four adult children and lives in Boulder Colorado. His wife allows him to ski 30-40 days a year. He is trained as a sommelier, a cook and a multi-engine, instrument pilot though he has never practiced sommelier skills while flying.

CPSIA information can be obtained at www.ICGtesting.com
Printed in the USA
LVOW10s0820161015

458520LV00004B/4/P